"History books that contain no lies are extremely dull"

Anatole France 1844-1924

South Stoke Historical Society

Front cover illustration: painting by William Costiff (c.1856-1938) showing the southern end of The Street looking south towards the bridleway. Courtesy of Margaret Lane.

A South Stoke resident in the 1920s, a "Stoker"

SOUTH STOKE'S PAST

A MISCELLANY

CURATED BY

LINDA GATTO
JANET JONES
&
MICHAEL SAUNDERS

On behalf of
The South Stoke Historical Society

Published by:
TAVERNICUS PUBLISHING
CAVENDISH LODGE, BATH

First published in Great Britain in 2020 by Tavernicus Publishing

www.tavernicus.co.uk

A catalogue record for this book is available from the British Library

ISBN: 978-0-9564065-4-5

This book is dedicated to those members of the South Stoke Historical Society who have contributed to the recording of events, people and places which make up this miscellany. This book has been in the making for over thirty years and many hands have put pen to paper, typed from manuscripts and researched photo archives. Many of these volunteers are no longer with us and this is for them.

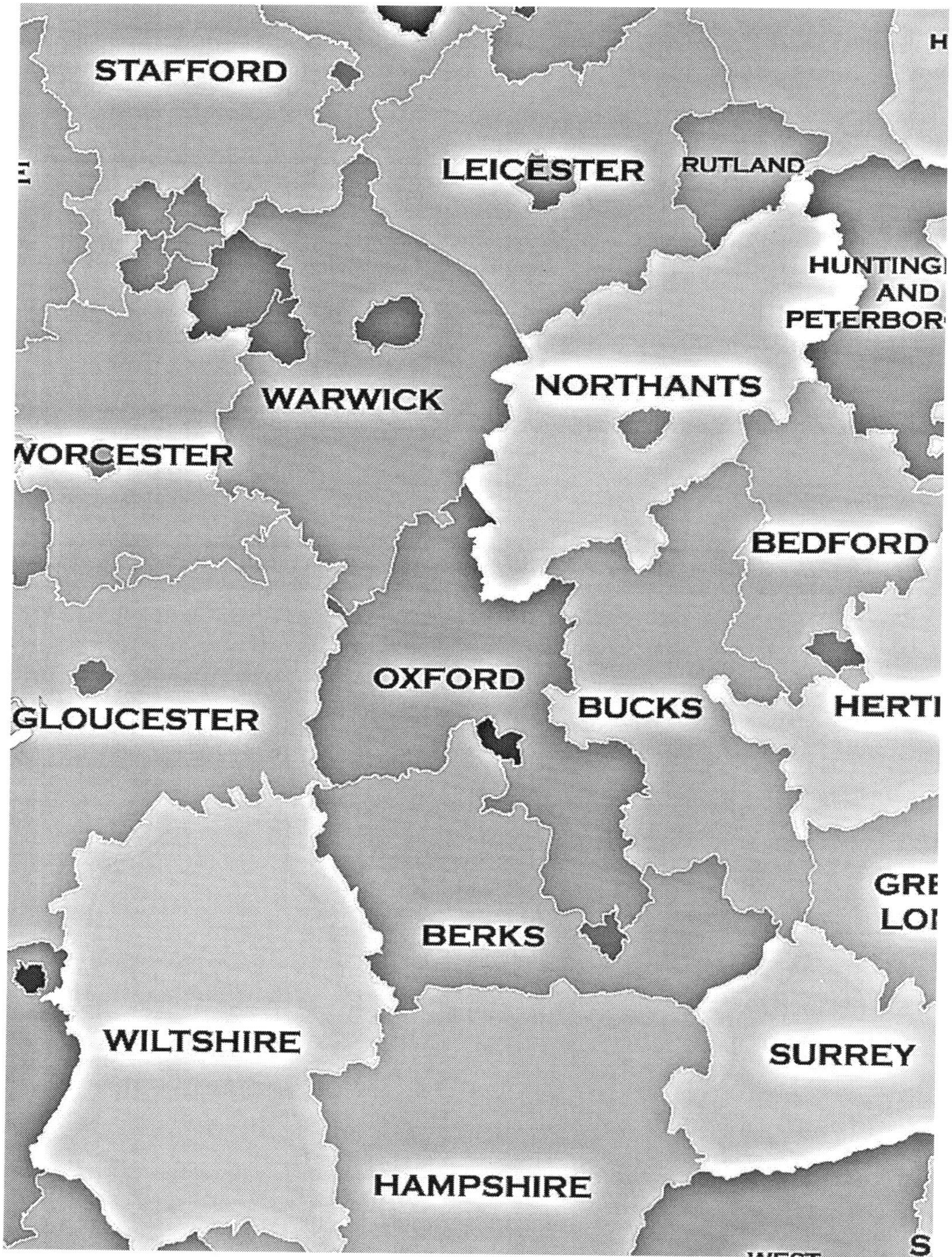

Map showing the counties surrounding Oxfordshire

Oxfordshire showing the ancient parish boundary of South Stoke cum Woodcote

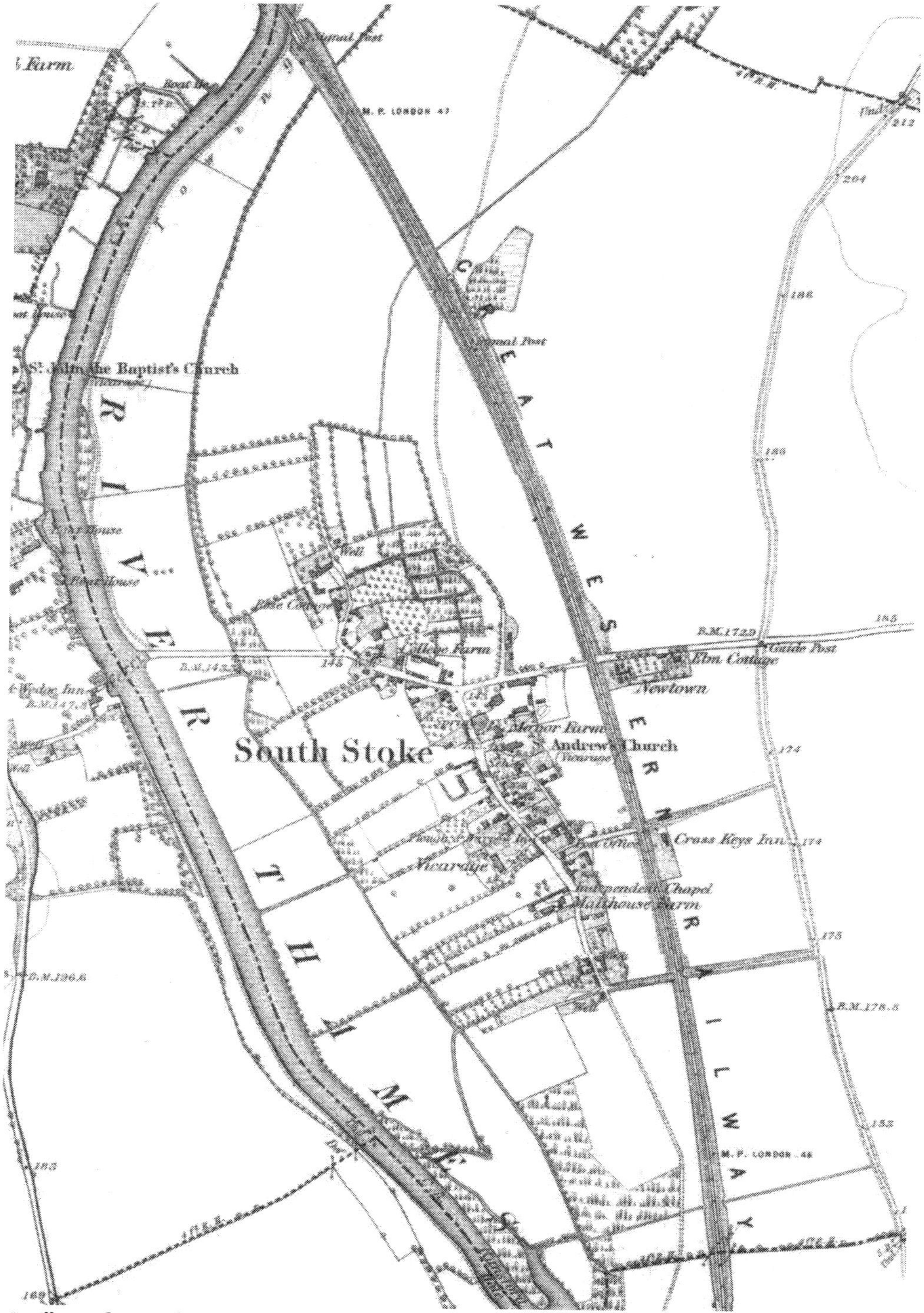

OS 6" to the mile map of South Stoke in1877 bounded by the river & railway

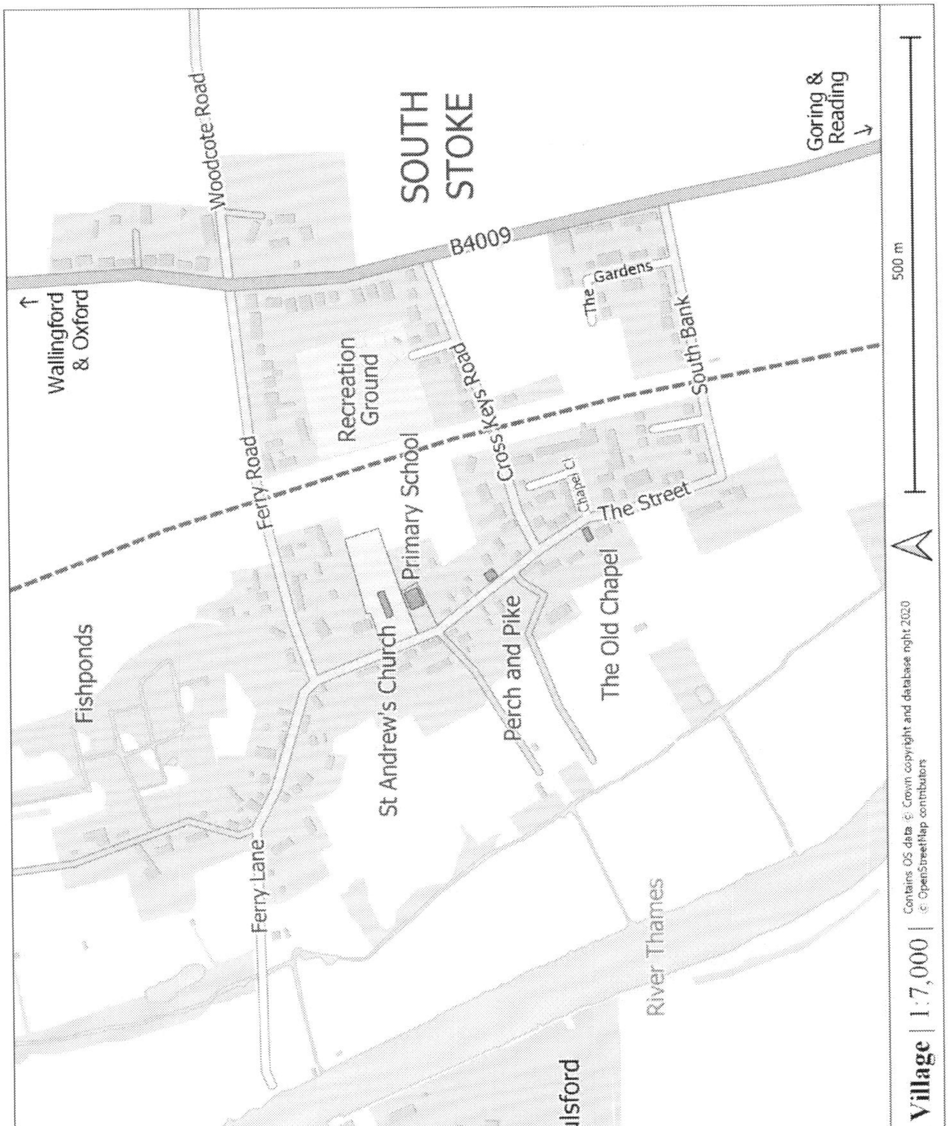

The village of South Stoke today bordering the River Thames to the west. The railway appears to cut the village in two but until the beginning of the 19th century there were little or no dwellings to the east of the railway line.

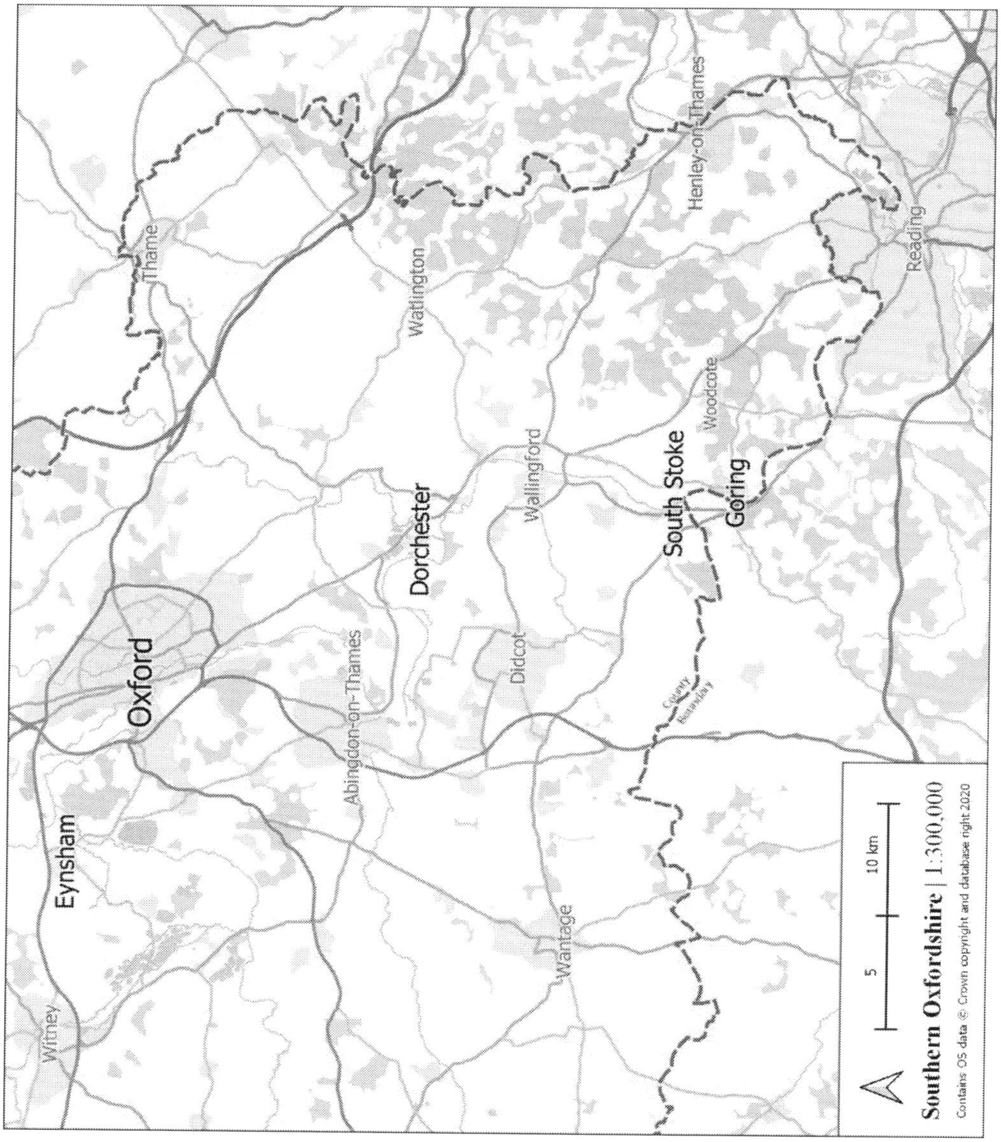

Modern day map showing the southern county boundary and the surrounding area of South Stoke and Woodcote.

CONTENTS:

FOREWORD

South Stoke in Oxfordshire is a Thameside village close to the Goring Gap on the east side of the river which runs north south at this point, with Wallingford to the north and Goring-on-Thames to the south. The village lies in the heart of a rural landscape and was once solely a farming community with deep connections to the church. Much has changed and some of that evolution is embodied in the pages of this book.

The quotation on the very first page gets our equaliser in first as the contents of this book are the result of the work of many contributors over the last thirty years. The Society has had a number of lives and with each incarnation a new group has picked up the baton from where the previous group left off. This particular incarnation began in 2017 and there had been previous South Stoke residents who had met to progress the writing of the history of the village, starting in 1986 when the society was founded. The society first published *"South Stoke Trade and Traders"* in 1988 and then subsequently in 1991 mounted an exhibition *"South Stoke: a Village History"* at the Wallingford Museum. These early initiatives formed the basis of the first draft of a book on the history of South Stoke. As group members changed over the years the initial draft evolved and re-evolved as a result; at the start of this revival there were three versions of a prospective publication each built on the previous attempts.

Only one of the earlier versions was available in electronic form so the first task was to digitise the soft copies. A society member had the knowledge and skill of how to do this which became our starting point. However, to get to first base it was necessary to combine the versions of the prospective book and then to eliminate duplications. As these versions were in black folders the task became known as producing The Black Book, which became the working title. After many hours of editing and compiling the Black Book it then became obvious that this mountain climb had hardly left the foothills.

In order to publish a book of historical essays and recollections the first task was to verify as much as possible of the contents and to provide source information to readers. Given that many of the contributors had died or moved away, the records for sources were sadly lacking, even non-existent. Many hours have been spent in archives to try to create a work which, whilst not academic in nature is, to the greatest extent possible, a true record. That said, there will be certain unverifiable content, in the nature of personal recollections, which is included in good faith. As already said, "History books that contain no lies are extremely dull".

The Black Book became the true starting point for this book. Once verification of the compiled book had been completed, it became clear that there was much content to add as many years had passed since the first thoughts had been put to paper. Not only that, the internet and the digital camera had meanwhile become part of daily life and whole new vistas opened up. The internet became a major source of information, maps and images. In addition, the society included a number of members with specialist knowledge which led to wholly new chapters or significant upgrades to the content of the earlier work. Hence this book should not be seen as a chronological history of South Stoke but more a collection of essays on selected topics which, taken together, give a picture of village life as it has evolved. As the contributors are many, the form of the essays is personal to the writers or editors and no attempt has been made to produce a harmonised style. There will be some duplication in the essays or chapters as there is an inevitable cross over between subjects. Hence, this is a book to dip into rather than to read sequentially; it is a miscellany.

This book is parochial in its true sense as it is the story of the small parish of South Stoke which has been a settlement for centuries. The population has never exceeded 1000 and today is around 500. Although surrounded by farmland, the consolidation and mechanisation of the local farms means that the community has transformed in the last couple of generations. Today, the village has its fair share of commuters as connections to London by rail are excellent but there is a vibrant local spirit as we have a church, a school, a pub, a community shop, a village recreation ground, numerous societies and we are lucky to live in an Area of Outstanding Natural Beauty. We hope you enjoy the tour.

The Curators

ACKNOWLEDGEMENTS

The committee of the society has worked tirelessly to bring the Black Book to publication. We must thank Sarah Phipps (President), as the guiding light of the earlier committees, for keeping the flame alight and protecting the archive records which became our starting point. Lis Harrison took over the role of archivist and has made a very valuable contribution, ably supported by Alan Harrison as treasurer. Roger Guiver set up the initial technology for the society. Previous group members had left us with a legacy of funds to revive the society, not just for the purpose of this book, but to campaign for new members, set up meetings with guest speakers and to organise outings.

The membership has grown to over forty and we are supported by some members of the Goring Gap History Society. Many villagers of long standing have contributed photographs and memories to this book. There have also been some contributions of note. Terry Jones digitised the soft copies into one version and eliminated much of the duplication. Without that wizardry this book would still be in box files. Certain chapters have either been written from scratch or edited beyond recognition. Special mentions therefore to Rod Payne for the Railway chapter and Lady Clothier for the Roads and River chapters. The expertise is acknowledged of Micky Connors for Ale and Beer, Martin Bullock for Agriculture, Robert Small for Bellringing and Geoff Ward for assisting with maps. Map assistance was also provided by Ashley Downend from the GIS Team at South Oxfordshire & Vale of White Horse District Councils. Last but not least, Jane Newton who did an exceptional job proof reading the first draft of this book.

The first draft of the Black Book contained the following acknowledgements which must be repeated here for without the sources and the volunteers this book would still be just an aspiration.

"Written:- Kelly's Directory; Register of Baptisms, Marriages and Deaths; Census return, 1841; Enclosure award, 1843; Tithe award, 1846,; Tithe map, 1853; the Eynsham Cartularies; Christ Church Archives; Victoria County History (VCH); the Bullock Family Scrap Book; The Women's Institute Village Scrap Books; Memories of the Happy Circle (over 60s club); The History of Higgs (or Higges) South Stoke, Oxon and Thatcham by William Miller Higgs; and Eynsham Abbey by Richard Gordon.

Verbal:- Frank and June Bullock; Brian Cooke; Ray Allum; Eric and Esther Small; Nancy Fox; Jessie and Aubrey Dawe; Peggy Pepler. And members of the committee, Sarah Phipps, Chairman; Hanmer Dickson; Dennis Greenland; Linda Gatto; Sheridan Thynne; Katherine Verrill; Ann and Greg Dean, and past members Rod Sharman, Chairman; Pat and John Dando; Geoffrey Tozer; Frank Onians; George Abdy; Tom Martin; Lorna Mearns; John and Audrey Martin; Mike Armstrong; Richard Fearn; Martin Bullock; all inspired by Jack Fothergill-Cooke."

CHAPTER 1

SOUTH STOKE- CUM-WOODCOTE TIMELINE OF EVENTS

Based on parish records and published sources.

634 St Birinus was Bishop of Dorchester.

1005 Eynsham Abbey was founded.

1086 The Domesday Book referred to the village as *"Stoch"* being *"part of the Bishop of Lincoln's manor of Dorchester."*

1094 South Stoke was given to Eynsham Abbey by the Bishop of Lincoln.

1109 King Henry I confirmed the possessions of Eynsham Abbey already held by them. South Stoke and Woodcote amongst some other parishes were gained in exchange for possessions lost at Stow near Lincoln.

1539 The dissolution of Eynsham Abbey.

1546 Christ Church, Oxford, was founded by King Henry VIII and South Stoke was granted to it as one of its endowments.

1552 There were "four belles" recorded in Edward VI's reign.

1600 The first Parish Register (on parchment) opened for Marriages, Baptisms and Burials, but earlier entries, back to 1557 and in some cases 1552, were copied into it "*out of the old Book*" by the Vicar - Hilary Fishwick.

1602 Knapp's Charity founded. £1 per year, equally divided between South Stoke and Woodcote, towards clothing the poor.

1609 Four of the bells at St Andrew's Church were recast during
1616 the reigns of James I and his son Charles I.
1622
1633

1659 The Doctor's Gift founded (Dr. Griffith Higgs). £3 per year to six poor families at South Stoke, and £2 per year to six poor families at Woodcote.

1675 Great Coat Charity founded. £5 per year to provide five coats to five poor men. One at South Stoke, two at Woodcote, and two at Checkendon, by the will of Henry Parslow.

1715 In the will of Mrs Susannah Newman land was given worth £10 per year to build a charity school in Woodcote for 10 poor children. Six were to come from the South Stoke parish and four from Checkendon.

1716 A new bell was installed in the reign of George I.

1724 The Allnutt's Charity founded. Almshouses and a school for boys at Goring Heath providing one place each for a South Stoke poor man and poor child.

1801 The combined population of South Stoke cum Woodcote was 564.

1811 The combined population of South Stoke cum Woodcote was 645.

1813 Separate Registers for Baptisms, Marriages and Burials opened. Printed forms, with the name of the officiating minister and other information in each case.

1820 The Congregational Chapel, belonging to the Countess of Huntingdon's Connexion, was built at South Stoke at a cost of nearly £332.

1821 The combined population of South Stoke cum Woodcote was 739.

1831 The total number of inhabitants in the parish was 751.

1831 The Blanket Charity was founded. The income from £100 in 3% Annuities for the relief of the poor at South Stoke and Woodcote equally, by the will of Mrs Jane Williams of Bourton on the Hill, Gloucestershire.

1834 The Poor Law Amendment Act provided for Union Workhouses to be built throughout the country. Henceforth the poor of South Stoke would be dealt with at the Wallingford Union Workhouse.

1838-1840	Construction of the section of Brunel's Great Western Railway that runs through the parish of South Stoke.
1840	The first recorded school building was erected at South Stoke. The Curate, Reverend John Trollope was the instigator of this enterprise.
1841	There were 405 inhabitants at South Stoke and 502 at Woodcote.
1845	The comparative trials between Brunel's broad gauge or the more popular narrow gauge ran through South Stoke.
1851	The combined population of South Stoke and Woodcote was 856.
1853	The land surrounding South Stoke including the common land was enclosed at this time by Act of Parliament.
1861	There were 360 inhabitants at South Stoke and 450 at Woodcote.
1862	A new school was built at South Stoke to replace the 22 year old school building. The cost was £520.
1869	The Vicarage at South Stoke was built by the Reverend Nind. The cost was £2000.
1871	There were 331 inhabitants at South Stoke and 431 at Woodcote.

1876 Claxson's Charity founded. The income was to provide clothing for the poor of Woodcote.

1881 The village stocks were removed from the west end of the present churchyard adjoining The Street.

1881 The total number of inhabitants at South Stoke and Woodcote was 838.

1881 A fifth bell was installed at South Stoke Church during Queen Victoria's reign.

1885 The Temperance Hall was built.

1887 Celebrations at South Stoke for Queen Victoria's Jubilee included dinner for 300 in a barn lent by Messrs J and G Bullock and tea at 6 pm.

1891 The total number of inhabitants at South Stoke and Woodcote was 717.

1896 About this time the Temperance Hall had been given over to the Parish Council with a view to resiting it in its present position (adjacent to the Bier Path), courtesy of Christ Church.

1901 The combined population of South Stoke cum Woodcote was 780.

1905 The great fire in South Stoke village.

1906 South Stoke school buildings and land let to Oxfordshire County Council (as the local education authority) for 21 years at 10/- (50p) per year by the Vicar and Churchwardens and incrementally thereafter.

1911 Population of South Stoke was only 320 according to the Licensing Authority in Oxford.

1918 13th November the first Women's Institute was held in the village. The President was Mrs Clarke.

1920 South Stoke War memorial was erected. The cost was £59/4/-, built by Honeybone and Son of Wallingford. The Church Clock was also installed in the same year.

1920 A sixth bell at South Stoke Church was given by Alfred D'Oyly Nind, the Vicar's brother, in memory of the men of South Stoke and Woodcote who fell in the Great War. George V was monarch.

1937 The Lych Gate at the entrance to South Stoke Churchyard was erected in memory of H G Nind where the stocks were once located.

1939 Combined population of South Stoke and Woodcote was 879.

1952 South Stoke and Woodcote became separate civil Parishes.

1967 The Cross Keys pub closed, leaving the Perch and Pike the only remaining pub in the village.

1976 The Chapel closed for worship.

1977 Queen Elizabeth II's Silver Jubilee celebrations.

1984 St. Andrew's Church became a United Benefice with St. Thomas of Canterbury's Church in Goring

2000 Millennium celebrations and the building of a slipway at the bottom of Ferry Lane.

2001 The population of South Stoke only, was 458.

2002 Queen Elizabeth II's Golden Jubilee.

2007 South Stoke and Goring churches united with St. Mary's Church at Streatley.

2011 The population of South Stoke was 507.

2012 Grants and fund-raising enabled a Community Shop and new play equipment to be erected on the Recreation Ground.

2015 Railway electrification took place and gantries were erected along the line through South Stoke.

2017 Fund raising enabled church clock winding equipment to be electrified, thus avoiding the need for manual winding.

2018 Population of South Stoke estimated at 516.

2018 The Women's Institute Centenary with Mrs Rita Mann as President.

2020 VE Day celebrations cancelled due to the corona virus pandemic.

Detail of the whole parish of South Stoke cum Woodcote from the Thomas Jefferys' map of 1767. South Stoke is situated in the north west of the parish and "Woodicot" in the south east.

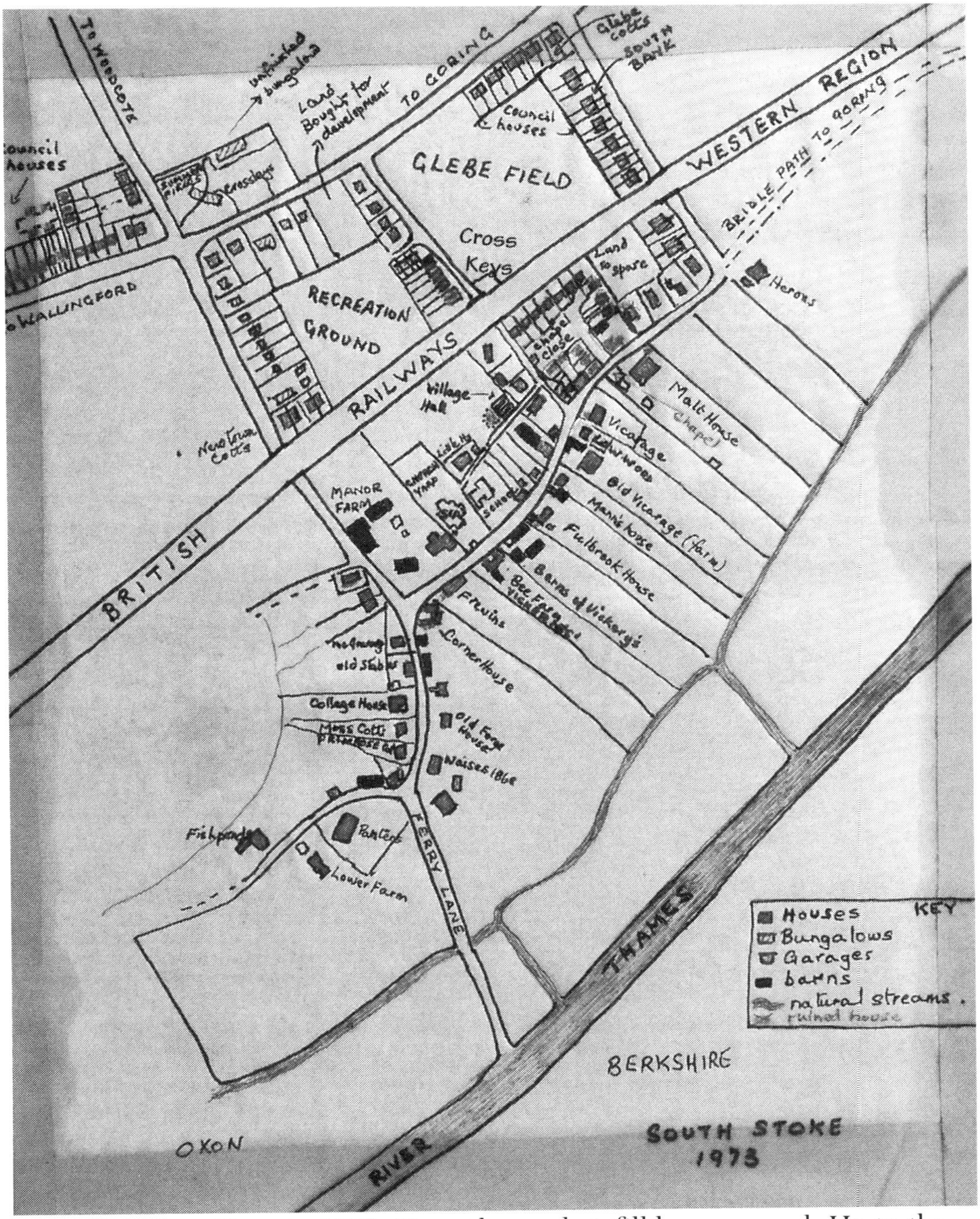

South Stoke village in 1973. Since then only infill has occurred. Up to the early 20th century most of the houses were below the railway line.

St Andrew's Church 1902

St Andrew's Church today with the 1920 tower clock and the 1937 lych gate

CHAPTER 2

THE PARISH OF SOUTH STOKE AND THE CHURCH OF ST. ANDREW

A church is thought to have stood in South Stoke for nearly 900 years, with the village itself dating from Anglo-Saxon times. The pre-Conquest history of South Stoke is obscure; but it has long had links with Dorchester, being given to the Saxon Bishop of that see prior to the 10th century. The first bishop was St. Birinus in 634, and the last Saxon prelate died in 1067.

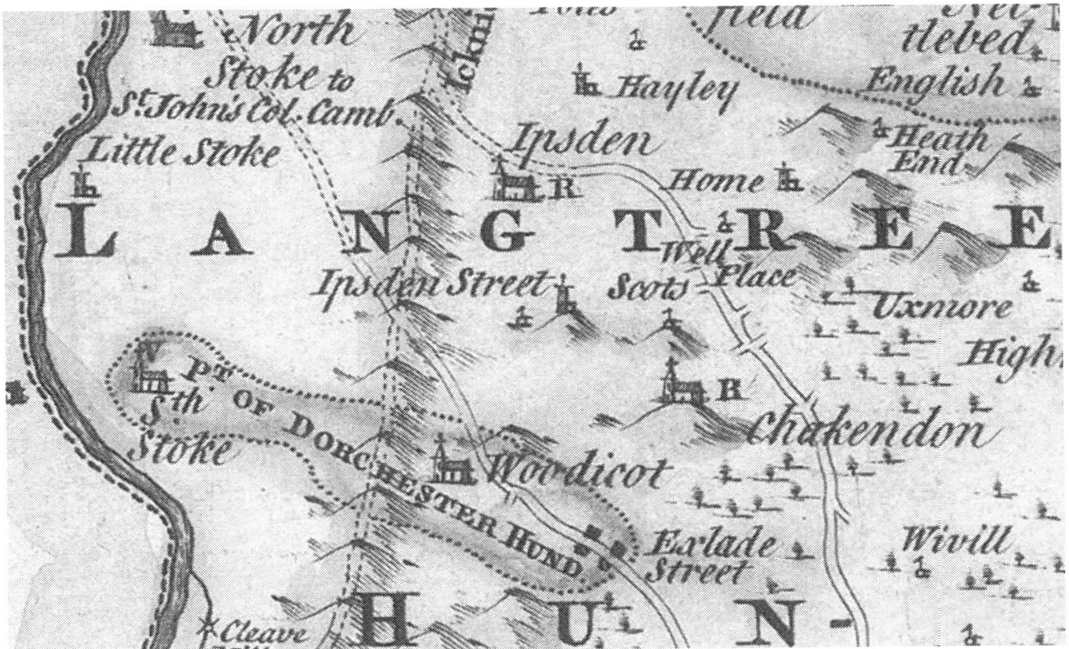

1760 map by Kitchin showing South Stoke in the Dorchester Hundred completely surrounded by the Langtree Hundred

The see was then given to the Norman Bishop Remigius, who had come over with William the Conqueror to England; and who, it was said, so much appreciated the eels that South Stoke was able to supply to his table[1] that he persuaded King William to let the parish remain for all time within the Dorchester Hundred. This story cannot be verified but it is indeed the situation even today that the parish is a Dorchester Hundred enclave within the Langtree Hundred. Bishop Remigius left his seat in Dorchester in 1072 heading northwards to set up in Lincoln. At that time his bishopric covered a vast area (the Thames to Yorkshire) and Dorchester was at its southern point.

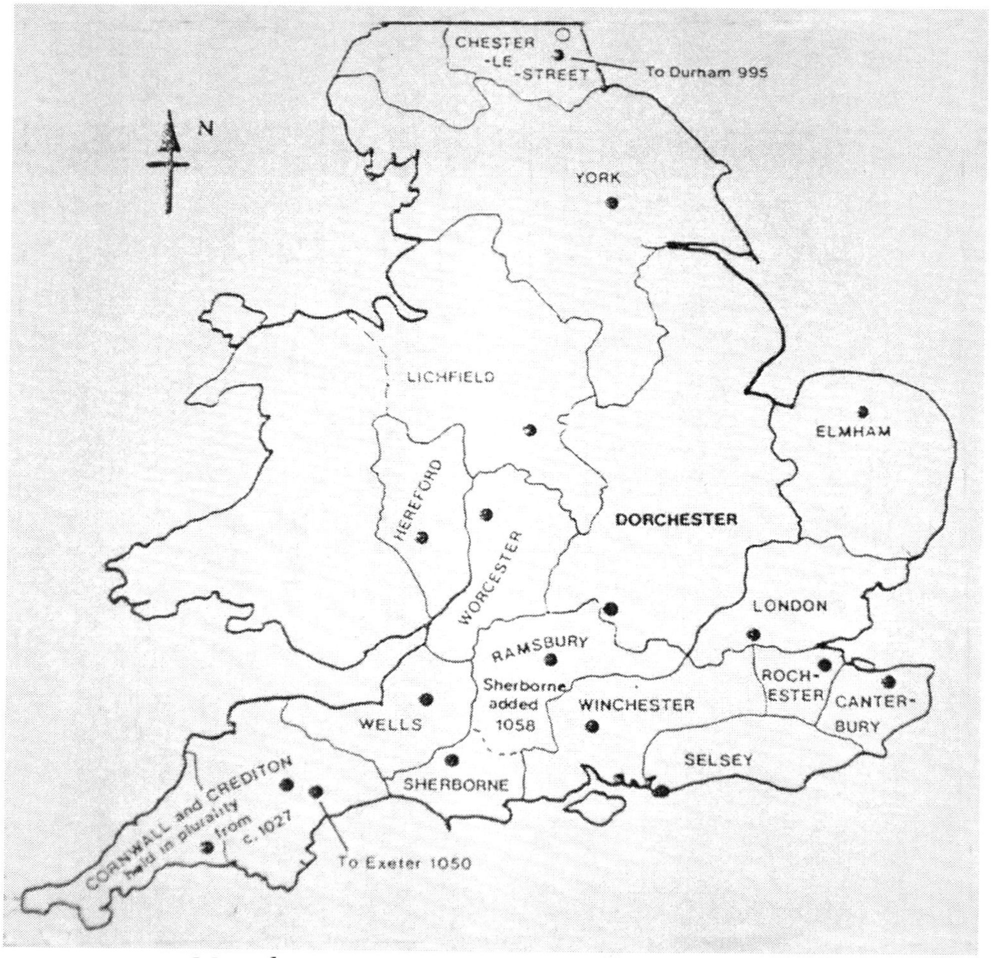

Map showing Diocesan Boundaries c.1090

He needed to be more centrally based in order to keep a watch over the Saxons. South Stoke, however, was still under his control. The village has been known by various names over time, Stoch and Bishops Stoke in the time of the bishop and Stoke Abbotes when given to Eynsham Abbey. More recently it was Stoke Abbas and finally South Stoke (to distinguish it from North Stoke).

It is of interest to note that St. Birinus, who brought Christianity to the West Saxons in 634 and who was responsible for building the first Saxon Cathedral at Dorchester, was also much concerned with the early parish boundaries, see below.

The Victoria County History records that "*a permanent memorial to the work of Birinus was the demarcation of ecclesiastical parish boundaries in south east Oxfordshire*". These parishes *"remained little changed to the*

present day and gave access to river and wooded hills"; thus ensuring that each parish had its fair share of river, meadow, arable and woodland.

Such was the case until recently, with the ecclesiastical parish of South Stoke-cum-Woodcote having always been long and narrow, running in a strip up from the Thames to include Woodcote and the hamlet of Exlade Street. South Stoke with its church and Woodcote with its chapel have long been known as the downhill and uphill parts of the parish, being divided by the line of the Icknield Way. In 1952, with the rapid growth of Woodcote as a commuter centre for Reading, it was decided that separate civil parishes for Woodcote and South Stoke should be created, and this was then done with the boundary following the old demarcation line between the downhill and uphill sections. The ecclesiastical parish of South Stoke-cum-Woodcote however remained unchanged, and it was not until 1981 that the church authorities followed suit: Woodcote was then linked with Checkendon and Stoke Row to form the Langtree Team Ministry, leaving South Stoke as a separate parish, with the proposal that in due course it would be linked to Goring to form the new United Benefice of Goring with South Stoke. This eventually took place and further amalgamation occurred in 2007 when the United Benefice was joined with Streatley. Thus a break was made in the ancient arrangement of the narrow strip parish running uphill from the Thames.

St. Birinus, whilst Bishop of Dorchester in the 7th century, *"built and dedicated several churches and brought many people to God*".[2] However, there is no mention in the 1086 Domesday entry of a church at South Stoke. This is not significant as Domesday did not give a complete record of all churches. It is known that South Stoke was given to Eynsham Abbey by Bishop Robert Bloet of Lincoln around

1094, as part of the property exchanged for the church of Stow St. Mary, Lincolnshire. The estate, together with Woodcote, was confirmed to Eynsham by Henry I in 1109. It is further known that by 1190, when South Stoke and its church were confirmed to Eynsham Abbey by Bishop Hugh, that the church "had evidently been long in existence".[3] South Stoke was now a rectory in Eynsham Abbey's patronage, though still under the overlordship of the Bishop of Lincoln. The right of patronage or advowson gave a landowner the right to appoint a parish priest on his land, such a right being an old one dating from Anglo-Saxon times. The Abbot of Eynsham thus became responsible for appointing a rector (who retained the great tithes of corn, grain, hay and wood) or a locum vicar (who was granted the small tithes including vegetables and fruit). The Victoria County History indicates that "*the first recorded rector of Stoke, who appears soon after 1200, was named Ralph. He had a chaplain and lived in the parish, for he witnessed local deeds and his parsonage is mentioned about this time*".

In 1397 Pope Boniface IX gave Eynsham permission to serve South Stoke with a chaplain and to farm all its property without the Bishop of Lincoln's prior approval. Royal consent followed, provided that a vicarage was ordained, and thus in 1399 the church was formally appropriated to Eynsham Abbey and the Bishop's overlordship fell away. The purpose of such a vicarage being ordained for South Stoke was "*in order that divine service should be regularly held, the piety of the parishioners encouraged, and the cure of souls not neglected*". The church remained in the Abbey's possession until its dissolution in 1539 by Henry VIII. In 1546 the King granted all the Abbey's lands to Christ Church, Oxford[4] which continued the practice (begun by Eynsham in the 15th century) of leasing the manor but retaining the advowson (basically the right to appoint vicars).

South east view of St Andrew's 1880

By 1190 it was stated that the church at South Stoke "*had evidently long been in existence*". However in their "*Buildings of England: Oxfordshire*", Jennifer Sherwood and Nikolaus Pevsner describe St Andrew's as a "*13th century church much altered in the 14th century*". Obviously, the earlier church had been in need of renovation and in the early 13th century it was entirely rebuilt. In consequence it is a far more elegant church than it might have been if rebuilt earlier and is in the Gothic Early English style as opposed to the Romanesque style. Items of note include the 17th century memorial to Dr. Griffith Higgs, a benefactor to the village who was chaplain to Queen Elizabeth of Bohemia, eldest daughter of James I and sister to Charles I. Additionally there is a mediaeval font and the remains of a late 16th century Elizabethan wall painting, setting out the Ten Commandments.

A former vicar, H G Nind, tells how "*the church, standing on some of the highest ground in the village, with its peal of five bells, shows up well*"; and of how "*restored in 1857 it contains some fine old pointed arches*".

A booklet recording "A History and Guide to St Andrew's Church" can be found in the church itself and draws attention to the battlemented tower that was probably built early in the 15th century and houses the bells that ring regularly over the village in modern times.

The same south east view of St Andrew's in 2020

ENDNOTES:-

1. During Edward the Confessor's reign (1042-1066) South Stoke was worth 6 pounds but by 1086 the value had doubled and also *"it renders 12 sticks of eels"* (roughly a stick was about 25 eels). This would be payment in kind to the ecclesiastical institutions that could eat eels during Lent and whenever meat was banned on their calendar. Eels were not considered flesh.

2. Bede's Ecclesiastical History

3. Victoria County History

4. Founded earlier in 1525 as Cardinal College by Thomas Wolsey.

Detailed research was carried out in 1982/83 by the then Secretary to the South Stoke Parochial Church Council, Major J. Fothergill-Cooke who was greatly assisted by information provided by the County Archivist in Lincoln.

CHAPTER 3

BELLS AND BELLRINGING AT ST ANDREW'S CHURCH

Since the earliest days in this country, religion has played an important part in the lives of the people, especially in the region that became Oxfordshire where, whilst there were some 180 churches in the area by 1086, the number had grown to 260 by 1291. In South Stoke it seems that by 1190 the Church of St Andrew "had evidently long been in existence". This early church was however to disappear when it was entirely rebuilt in the early 13th century. In the 1530s Henry VIII broke with Rome, established the supremacy of State over the Church in England and ordered the dissolution of the monasteries. Amongst these was Eynsham Abbey, within the patronage of which that first church had been built at South Stoke. Both church and land now passed to Christ Church in Oxford. The Reformation was under way. In his booklet *"Discovering Bells and Bellringing"* (Shire Publications 1968, revised in 1988) the author John Camp has described how one result of this was *"the desecration of monastic buildings and abbeys throughout the land, which involved the destruction of much church property and the silencing or even removal of many church bells".*

Under Queen Elizabeth I (1558-1603) many desecrated churches were restored and bells in many bell-towers were re-hung. This would have pleased the Protestant martyr Bishop Latimer, who in

1552 had said that *"if all the bells of England were rung at one time there would scarcely be a single spot where a bell would not be heard"*. Later however, during the Commonwealth of 1649-1659, church festivals in general and the ringing of bells in particular were greatly discouraged. But, thereafter the overall restoration of churches provided the opportunity to improve on earlier changes in the hanging of church bells, and bells were now mounted on a whole wheel instead of the half wheel as previously.

In the words of John Camp *"a greater degree of control was now possible, and the swing of the bell could be slowed down or speeded up with the help of the rope"*. But there was still no way by which the bell's movement could be halted at will or restarted equally quickly. This is where the introduction of the slider and stay made this feasible. It was now possible to set the bell in the upside down position. Imagine a clock face. When ringing, a bell swings from balance point to balance point, ie the bell swings fully clockwise from 12:00 to 12:00 then likewise in the anticlockwise direction. If the ringer now wished to set the bell this was made possible by allowing the bell to gently go over the balance to the 11:00 or 1:00 positions thereby setting the bell in the upside down position using the stay and slider to fulfil this act. This was the precursor to all modern day ringing from call changes to method ringing now known as full circle ringing. It is of interest to note that bellringing now remained confined to the established Protestant churches, since for the next 300 years Catholic churches were not allowed to have any bells at all, whilst the non-conformist chapels of later years normally only had the one bell.

To revert however to the earliest days of the church in South Stoke. In those times churches had at least one bell, as was the case with South Stoke's sanctus bell, both to summon the faithful to prayer and to warn of possible disasters or unfriendly actions. As John Camp has written, *"up to the 14th century such bells were normally hung on a simple spindle and chimed by pulling a rope attached to the spindle"*, although in some cases the bell, which was motionless, was rung by a simple rope attached to the clapper. However, it was the movement of the bell and not the clapper that became the normal practice in this country. After the 14th century, *"ringers began to experiment with new ways of hanging the bell so that greater control could be exercised"*. A first change was to mount the bell on a wooden quarter-wheel, the spindle serving as the axle and with the rope attached to the rim of the wheel. In due course a further improvement, which gave even more control, was to attach the bell to a half wheel. By the 16th century many churches had two or three bells mounted in this fashion.

W E Tate in his book *"The Parish Chest"* (C.U.P. 1946) has explained how, in those days, a church warden's duties embraced *"the fabric of the church and all therein"*, and of how he was especially enjoined to keep the belfry keys and to *"take care that bells were not rung without due cause"*; whilst his accounts often showed fees for bellringers and expenditures on bells and tower clocks. Parish records show that ringing took place *"on saints eves and Saturdays and for matins and nones"* and there are numerous separate entries of ringing on the greater festivals. Bells were also rung *"upon the entry to or departure from a parish of the reigning monarch"*. Likewise coronations, births of royal heirs, major victories in wars and other happy events *"were all celebrated in that truly English fashion, the ringers being encouraged by a plentiful supply of ale"*. There is no doubt that nothing can compare with bells in their impressiveness. Indeed the 17th century historian Thomas Fuller once wrote in his *"Worthies"* that England was called the ringing island, being renowned for possessing greater, more numerous and more tuneable bells that any country in Christendom.

The tower of St Andrew's Church was probably built in the early 15th century, with its single sanctus bell. A 1552 inventory, as ordered by Edward VI, shows *"4 belles in the steeple"*, with some doubt being expressed as to what had happened to the earlier sanctus bell. This seems to indicate that bellringing in the village would have commenced around that time. These four bells were not to last for long and were all replaced or recast in the early 17th century. The replacements were all cast in Reading, the first three by Henry Knight I and the last by Ellis Knight I.

The inscriptions on those bells, together with their respective weights (in cwts, qrs, and lbs) and diameter measurements (in inches) are as follows:

TENOR *"Henri Knight made this bell in ano 1609 Blessed be the name of the Lord".*

9-2-0 and 38 ins.

FIFTH *"Henri Knight made mee ano 1616".*

7-0-0 and 33 ins.

SECOND *"Henri Knight made mee 1622 IH IW BH IH GH / WT AH BC".*

4-3-0 and 27 1/2 ins.

THIRD *"Feare God 1633".*

5-1-0 and 29 1/2 ins.

To these four another bell was added in 1716.

FOURTH *"William Higgs & William Claxson CW Will Rob Cor 1716".*

Weight and size unknown.

In 1881 it became necessary to recast one of the bells, replace the fourth and overhaul the others. A new bell (paid for by public subscription) was then ordered and installed, with the inscription:

"Mears & Stainbank, Founders, London. 1881

Revd P H Nind, Vicar. John Bullock, Churchwarden".

6-1-10 and 31 1/2 ins.

Philip Nind was in his 75th year and celebrating his golden wedding anniversary. John Bullock, together with his brother worked Manor Farm. He had been a churchwarden for seven years and was to remain in post for another 35 years until his death in 1916. This gave the tower a ring of five bells.

In 1920 the bells were again overhauled, tuned and the fourth recast. A new frame and fittings were installed at the same time. All work being carried out again by Mears & Stainbank.

In that same year the youngest brother of the then vicar, H G Nind, presented the last or treble bell, inscribed:

"Mears & Stainbank, Founders, London

To the Memory of the Men of the joint Parish of South Stoke and Woodcote,

who fell in the Great War, 1914-1919.

Alfred D'Oyly Nind gave me, 1920"

4-0-10 and 26 1/2 ins.

Treble bell with rope tied temporarily to hold clapper to side of bell whilst a learner practises (quietly)!

In 1965 all six bells were examined, and their clappers attended to, by Mears & Stainbank. Fourteen years later a further examination was carried out by the Oxford Diocesan Guild of Church Bellringers. This included the inspection of the Taylor iron main bell frame (found to be in good condition) and the three steel joists which enter the east and west walls. The mixed layout of the different sized bells was to ensure that no undue strain was imposed on the tower structure when all the bells were rung together. For the same reason, some bells swing in one direction and others in another. At this time the bells were hung on wooden blocks which required constant greasing and attention. The Guild suggested that all the bells might one day be rehung on roller bearings for smoother and easier ringing. This was achieved by late 1997.

The bells, from left to right, are number 2, 1(treble), 6 (tenor, clock chiming bell) and 5. Behind, in the left corner, are 4 and just the wooden wheel of bell 3. The wooden wheels take up the slack from the ringing chamber. The headstocks (the metal bars above each bell) swing with the bell and are each hung on two ball bearings within housings which in turn are bolted to the mainframe (horizontal bar in the foreground). The configuration of the bells help even out the strain on the tower walls.

Wanting to commemorate the 50th anniversary of the end of World War II and preparing bells throughout the land to ring in the Millennium provided the impetus and some funding to overhaul the bells yet again. Volunteers provided the labour for the mammoth task and White's of Appleton the expertise. A service of rededication was held on 17th January1998 and the bells were set fair to ring in the Millennium.

During the 18th and 19th centuries there was much friction between clergy and bellringers, which led to clergy taking little interest in bellringing or on spending money on bells or belfry. Indeed ringers were then regarded as layabouts and drunkards. The position however was to change in the latter half of the 19th century. In particular, 1871 brought the Rev. P H Nind from Woodcote to his newly built vicarage in South Stoke. Where there was already much ill-will between clergy and parishioners, the vicar's relocation did much to improve the situation. He appointed head ringers, who would decide on what should be rung at services, would train newcomers to the art and would be responsible for the regular attendance of bellringers and for their good behaviour. A copy of the 'Ringers' Rules' produced by Philip Nind around 1875 stresses the strict behaviour to be enforced in the belfry. This can still be seen in the belfry today (2020), and, as we have seen, he was in 1871 instrumental in getting a new bell provided by public subscription to replace an older one. The Parish Register records how, *"on Feb 18 1882, the new bell was placed in the belfry this day by Mr Frederick White ... after a delay of more than ten months. The cost was*

£28, raised by subscriptions in the neighbourhood. The first peal was rung on the evening of Feb 18th. P H Nind, Vicar".

By the end of the 19th century women were arriving in belfries, despite opposition from diehards. In 2020, a mixed band of ringers operates in the village but on the 12th August 2019 probably for the first time ever an all-female band rang for the Sunday service. Contrary to popular belief ringing does not require too much physical effort; what is needed is an orderly mind, a retentive memory and a good sense of timing.

From time to time muffled ringing is called for. This type of ringing is rung in most towers on Remembrance Sunday. This is achieved by placing a leather pad on one side of the clapper. This gives the bell a haunted sound on that stroke, the other side being left open as in day to day ringing. The only time full muffled ringing is allowed is upon the death of a monarch. In that instance a leather pad is also placed on the other side of the clapper. Half muffled ringing is becoming popular nowadays (2020) at funerals as is the tolling of the tenor bell to the age of the deceased.

In South Stoke the bellringers' chamber was originally on the ground floor of the Tower, which meant quite an interval of time between the pulling of the rope and the actual movement of the bell. However in 1962-63 the vestry was moved from its original position at the eastern end of the south aisle to the ground floor of the tower, when the bellringers' chamber was then moved to the first floor. Here the ropes of numbers 1 and 6 bells (the treble and tenor) hang on the north side, and those of numbers 2, 3, 4 and 5 in a semicircle on the south side. As a result a pull on the rope has an almost instantaneous effect on the bell. The second floor of the tower is the clock room, containing the clock which was given in 1920 in memory of the Rev. P H Nind (Vicar of South Stoke-cum-Woodcote from 1844-1886) by his surviving sons. This clock was religiously wound by hand crank every week. However, in 2017 funds were raised to fully automate the winding and timing of the clock and in 2020 the clock face was refurbished. The top floor is the actual belfry with its six bells. From the belfry there is access through a heavy trapdoor to the top of the tower, where there is a flagpole and weathervane. From here there is an excellent view of the whole village and its surrounding fields and meadows.

Before any ringing can start bells have to be 'rung up' from the hanging down position. This is achieved by swinging the bells higher and higher (using the ropes) until they are positioned upside down resting against the slider and stay. Another consideration before ringing is to disconnect the clock chimer, which normally strikes the tenor bell, otherwise it could become damaged.

Thereafter the ringer with firm, but gentle, even action, alternates between handstroke and backstroke. In both strokes the bell will ring as the ringer's hands pass the face. Having mastered these strokes, a beginner then has to learn the procedure for going faster and slower, and for setting the bell in its upward position when ringing stops. Thereafter the beginner must learn to take his/her place in ringing rounds, i.e. when bells all follow each other in sequence from the smallest to the largest. This requires considerable practice, as a ringer should only pull after the ringer he/she is following has pulled about half the length of their sally. The next technique to be learned is call-changing, when the captain will call upon two adjacent bells to change places in order of ringing. This enables a whole series of different changes to be made until the bells are finally called back to rounds. Call-changing became popular in the early 17th century.

The next step came when mathematical precision was brought to bellringing by one Fabian Stedman in the late 17th century, whereby the bells changed their order of ringing at every pull according to a laid-down pattern, without the need for calls. This was termed method ringing, with each method having a specific name, set out in writing on a board, which had then to be learned by heart by ringers. However, the basis of all method ringing, which had to be mastered first, was called Plain Hunting, when every bell changes by one place at every stroke, until it reaches last or first place where it must stay for two strokes. From Plain Hunting one can progress to Plain Bob. Thereafter, Grandsire Doubles and Stedman Doubles are some of the first methods to be learnt. Once a team has become proficient in the art of ringing it will often, as in the case of South Stoke, visit neighbouring churches to ring in their towers and thus gain further experience and confidence.

Throughout Oxfordshire bellringing has always been a most popular pastime, although the bells were quiet during the last world war and in the 2020 corona virus pandemic. Today church bells still provide the most arresting sound in a village, calling people to services, special events and other celebrations. In South Stoke itself, initial bellringing on four bells commenced in the 16th century, although more serious ringing would have taken place in the 17th century after those four bells were all recast and replaced. However, there is virtually no mention of bellringers or their activities over the years in the local parish registers. The following newspaper clipping from the Berkshire Chronicle of the 9th January 1904 reveals a little more of the bellringers' activities and who they were.

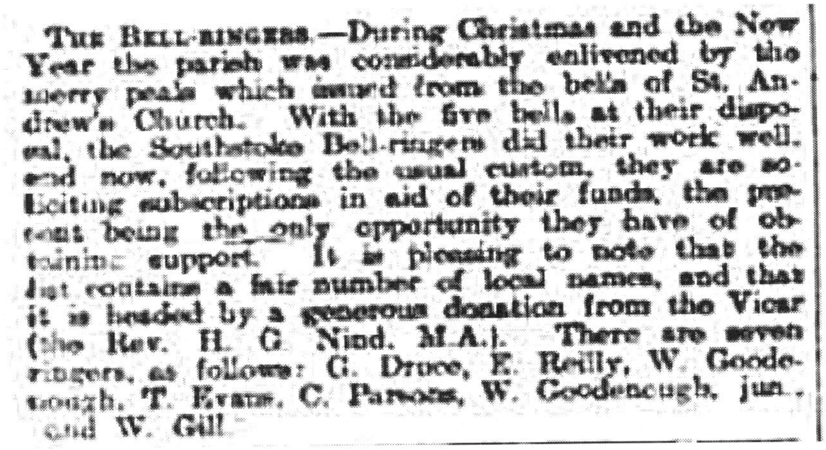
The Bell-ringers.—During Christmas and the New Year the parish was considerably enlivened by the merry peals which issued from the bells of St. Andrew's Church. With the five bells at their disposal, the Southstoke Bell-ringers did their work well, and now, following the usual custom, they are soliciting subscriptions in aid of their funds, the present being the only opportunity they have of obtaining support. It is pleasing to note that the list contains a fair number of local names, and that it is headed by a generous donation from the Vicar (the Rev. H. G. Nind, M.A.). There are seven ringers, as follows: G. Druce, E. Reilly, W. Goodenough, T. Evans, C. Parsons, W. Goodenough, jun., and W. Gill.

Otherwise only one specific name is recorded in 1922, when Sidney Kew is mentioned as captain of bellringers. In 1962 members of the Happy Circle in their *"Historical Recollections"* wrote that there is an unbroken history of bellringing in South Stoke by both men and women.

Our bellringers had the following tribute paid some years ago by a village poet:

The ringers of South Stoke are stalwart and strong folk

Ringing the changes in all their wide ranges

Of Service give warning betimes in the morning

All chiming at Even their music to Heaven

Their glad wedding peal sound joy we all feel

Whilst bidding us rest a single bell's best

After Sidney Kew the following, after many years of experience, became Captains of Bellringers in South Stoke: Fred Broadway, Laurie Pocock, Albert Pepler, Bill Pepler; and then in 1952, after 17 years of ringing, Ray Allum took over as Tower Captain. He was to serve until 1992, when he finally retired as Captain. Both Tim Eaton and Niall Ainscough acted as Captains in the 1990s until the Millennium when Robert Small took the reins. Over the years there have been many ringers but surprisingly few who were churchgoers. Unfortunately, no official records have been kept of their activities though The South Stoke Historical Society has a list of as many ringers that could be collected in living memory to the present.

CHAPTER 4

THE SOUTH STOKE CHAPEL
OF THE COUNTESS OF HUNTINGDON'S CONNEXION

Why was the Chapel built?

The establishment of the South Stoke Chapel must be viewed in the context of parish administration and the role of the Anglican Church within it. In addition, and likely related to it, was the growth of Dissent among those living in the parish.

During the 18th century, the Manorial Court gradually fell into disuse and the Church Vestry - with its Churchwardens, Overseers of the Poor, Surveyors of Highways and Constables, began to take over many civil duties. It collected tithes and rates, maintained roads and dealt with offenders. This incensed local farmers who had to pay the most in rates. The Vestry also ran into hostility over its conduct of local affairs, even though responsibility for the poor was removed from it in 1834 by the Poor Law Amendment Act. Its role in parish affairs was finally taken from it by the Local Government Act of 1894 which established parish councils within a system of rural and urban district councils. The Church was left thereafter to manage only its own affairs.

By 1815 the Vestry was at the height of its powers, with local rates at their highest level ever. No wonder there was dissatisfaction, which was compounded by various historical factors, such as the legacy of Puritan feelings from the Civil Wars and the practice of absentee vicars. Two vicars stand out in this connection namely, the Rev. Thomas Owen (vicar from 1790-1794) and his successor the Rev. John Williams (vicar from 1795-1844), strangers to South Stoke for over half a century.

Both these men appointed a succession of curates to run affairs in their absence, but it seems these curates were often refused local accommodation by dissatisfied farmers. In 1738 the vicar had reported only one Papist in the parish, together with three families of Presbyterians, and that "*no one professed to disregard religion*". But by 1815 the Victoria County History has indicated that the people of South Stoke "*were said to be generally dissenters*". In 1854 Philip Nind, who had followed John Williams as vicar, was reporting South Stoke to be "*a difficult place*", where he "*attributed deficiency to dissent and to evil and immoral example set by prominent farmers*". He went on to say that "*the whole of South Stoke with the exemption of about twenty are dissenters*". He blamed in the main "*the entire want of co-operation and assistance*" from the Christ Church authorities, "*whose estates are let to a violent opposer of the Church*" together with "*the opening of beer houses on Sundays.*" *The* "*violent opposer*" referred to was Isaac King, at that time lessee of both manorial rights and the Manor Farm.

Philip Nind also referred to the "*Independent Place of Worship*" in the village, which was being attended by these dissenters. This was the Chapel of the Countess of Huntingdon's Connexion. In his newspaper article Leslie North has indicated that this Chapel was built in 1820 (at the cost of £332) at the instigation of James Howes, Minister at the Goring Chapel (from 1814-56), where the South Stoke folk had worshipped "*till then*". The Goring Chapel had been built in the High Street in 1789 for the Countess of Huntingdon's

Connexion. The building today (2020) is used as the Goring Free Church Hall.

The Countess and her Connexion

Selena Hastings, Countess of Huntingdon, Anon., after a painting by J. Russell. © Museum of Bath Architecture - Bath Preservation Trust.

Who was the Countess of Huntingdon and what was her Connexion? Selina Shirley was born into a wealthy family on 24 August 1707 and was brought up with her two sisters at the family seat, Staunton Harold Hall, in Leicestershire. In 1728 she married Theophilus, 9th Earl of Huntingdon of Donington Park in the same county. She was to bear 4 sons and 3 daughters. Selina was a highly intelligent young woman, not enamoured with London society she preferred country life where she could help the poor and under privileged. She became deeply religious, particularly so after she recovered from a serious illness in 1738.

Together with her husband, Selina attended the first Methodist Society meetings in London in the late 1730s. Then, after her husband's death, she supported Wesley and Whitefield in the "work of the great revival". In 1748 she appointed the latter to be her chaplain and through him arranged meetings of Methodist ministers in her London town house. She was ably supported by her husband, perhaps a little reluctantly, until his death in 1746. Undoubtedly in her activities she was assisted, in one way or another, by her position as a peeress and with friends and acquaintances befitting that station.

Many of the Countess' friends found that they were driven from the Established Church owing to their evangelistic zeal and were forced to preach in the streets and in the countryside. Though still a member of the Church she decided to embark on building a series of chapels to serve as preaching stations.

After that, as the *"Encyclopaedia Britannica"* of 1910 makes clear,

"She spent her ample means in building chapels in different parts of England and appointed Ministers to officiate in them, under the impression that as a Peeress she had the right to employ as many chaplains as she pleased".

The first of the Countess' chapels built in North Street in Brighton opened in 1761.This was followed by Wivelsfield in Sussex and a third in Tunbridge Wells. The fourth chapel in Lewes was opened in 1765. All these chapels were administered by Church of England clergymen employed by Selina until these were replaced by students from her own Theological College at Treveca House near Talgarth in Wales set up in 1768. Over the years she was to spend £100,000 in "*the cause of religion*", a considerable sum of money at that time.

The interesting point is that the chapels and their officiating priests or ministers were theoretically still part of the Established Church. This caused a problem which came to a head in 1779 with the opening of the Spa Fields chapel in London. The local Church of England vicar objected to the presence of the chapel countered by Selena in a court case that she was entitled to appoint as many chaplains as she liked. However, it was deemed by the local Consistorial Court that her chaplains would have to be registered under the 1689 Toleration Act, a step that placed her and her chaplains legally among the Dissenters.

Henceforth her chapels, which had hitherto been part of the Church of England, were now registered as a sect known as the Countess of Huntingdon's Connexion as from 1781 with its own 15 Articles of Faith.

Until her death in London in 1791, the Countess "*continued to exercise an active and even autocratic superintendence over her chapels and chaplains"*. Her 64 chapels and colleges had become by 1910, 44 chapels and mission stations, with 2400 communicants under 26 ordained pastors. However, by 1965 the number of buildings had been reduced to 37, governed by nine trustees. By 1958 membership of the South Stoke Chapel was about 12.

Building the South Stoke Chapel and its Founders

Further information as to how the South Stoke Chapel came to be built is available in an old Indenture of 17th January 1821, which was and still is (2020) in the possession of the owners of the Malt House, of which the one time Chapel is now part. This document makes it clear that a certain Thomas Panter of South Stoke, who had;

"lately erected and built at his own expense a Chapel or Meeting House, which is now used and set apart as a place of religious worship for a Congregation of Protestant Dissenters ... hath agreed to vest the same ... in trust for the said congregation ... in consideration of the sum of two hundred pounds of good and lawful money ... to be raised by a subscription made for that purpose by the congregation and other friends and also in consideration of the sum of ten shillings by each of the said parties hereto paid to the said Thomas Panter."

Accordingly the Indenture was made out between Thomas Panter and the Rev. James Howes, Minister of Goring; with the added signatories of eight prominent South Stoke farmers, and fourteen other persons from Goring, Moulsford, Cholsey, Basildon and Ashampstead, described respectively as farmers, yeomen, fishermen, ferryman, wheelwright, carpenter and maltster. These 22 persons were clearly worshippers at the Chapel in Goring, and were concerned with the planning and building of the new Chapel at South Stoke. This Chapel was now made over to the Goring Minister and to themselves,

" ... *Upon trust ... to be used as a Place of Meeting for the Worship of Almighty God and the Administration of the Sacraments by a Congregation of Protestant Dissenters, who believe in and maintain the articles of faith compiled by the Reverend Assembly of Diviners, convened for that purpose at Westminster in 1643*".

The land on which Thomas Panter built his Chapel in 1820 had been made over to him in 1796 as part of the Malt House property, and the same indenture indicates that there had been some ten previous owners of the property going back to one Barton Day in 1706. The latter was clearly a well-to-do local farmer, who lived between 1662-1743 and was a descendant of Walter Barton, who was Lord of the Manor in 1536. Walter Barton was succeeded by his nephew, Griffith Barton, one of whose descendants was the well-known South Stoke personality and benefactor Griffith Higgs (1589-1659). Certainly the Barton Day family is well commemorated today by a number of tombstones in the churchyard, and especially by a fine chest tomb.

But what do we know of Thomas Panter and the eight other signatories to the Indenture making over the Chapel to Minister Howes? Thomas Panter himself (1764-1851) was a prominent local farmer and for many years, up to 1827, an Overseer of the Poor; also, at one time the Surveyor of Highways. The others were also well known contemporary figures, the first being the infamous Isaac King (1781-1865) who took on the lease of Manor Farm in 1831 and became a leading farmer and local personality. He was for several years both Churchwarden and Overseer of the Poor, as well as being a leading dissenter. He was a close colleague of Thomas Panter and the others, and was closely associated in the planning and construction of the Chapel and its handover to the Countess of Huntingdon's Connexion. On his death he was to leave £500 to the Chapel, as did his son after him. The King family all lie buried on the north side of the churchyard (reserved in those days for dissenters) as do members of the Panter family.

Interestingly, a third generation Isaac King (1845-1926) was also to cause controversy in the village when, as Leslie North has recorded;

"*In 1880 he raised a public subscription to erect a wood and iron Hall on his land* (on Cross Keys Road just west of the railway*) to promote gospel temperance and religious truth*".

When this Hall was built and opened in 1885 "*it caused controversy, with villagers wanting to use the building differently*". It seems the local people wanted to use it for more general social purposes, with King insisting it be used for religious and temperance purposes only. As Leslie North has put it: "*An independent crowd the South Stoke-ers!*". As a result of this dispute Christ Church subsequently agreed to make available, for a nominal sum, a suitable plot of land on another site, on which a Village Hall was erected early in the 20th century and where the present Hall still stands.

The next signatory was William Curtis, who too had been a Church Warden, Overseer of the Poor and a Surveyor of Highways for various periods up to 1802. He was followed by William Newell, who was also an Overseer of the Poor from 1897-98 and a local blacksmith. Then came Benjamin Panter, another member of that well-known farming family, whose forebears in South Stoke go back some 200 years. Indeed until recently, there was still a house in the village known by that name. Benjamin Panter too was an Overseer of the Poor, between 1805-06. The next signature after his was that of Richard Woodward, another local farmer and himself an Overseer of the Poor, from 1820 to 1823. His name also appears in an old Rate Book as being, in 1838, the occupier of the Malt House (owner Thomas Panter) and assessed at £25 for poor relief. Thereafter, follow the names of Thomas Higgs, William Moulden and William Panter, all described in old records as yeoman.

Thomas Higgs had also been an Overseer of the Poor, his last recorded spell of duty being from 1817-18, and he came from another well-known South Stoke family going back some 300 years. Of William Moulden little is known and he does not appear to have engaged himself in any civic duty, apart from the affairs of the Chapel. The last signatory however, William Panter, was both an Overseer of the Poor from 1800-02 and Churchwarden from 1802-07. It is somewhat strange that all these persons should have taken such an active part in the affairs of the Vestry of the Established Church, whilst at the same time being prominent dissenters. No doubt they felt that, as prominent and influential citizens they had a part to play in local affairs. But Vestry meetings must have been difficult ones in those days!

Later developments

Relationships between Church and Chapel goers were eventually to become quite amicable, with each having its adherents in the village and respecting the other. In 1961 local members of the Happy Circle Club put together some "*Memories of South Stoke*" and recorded that, during the Nind era, *"both Church and Chapel were vital and happy influences in the lives of the villagers"*, with their children attending Sunday School at both places of worship. Indeed, there were some people who still remembered going to Sunday Morning Service at the Chapel and Evening Service at the Church (after the Vicar had returned from Woodcote) with, as mentioned, children going to school at both places.

In 1903 an article in the Berks and Oxon Advertiser describes a service to commemorate the renovation of the Chapel, when the Rev. Pitt, pastor of Goring and South Stoke Chapels, said to the congregation that the South Stoke chapel had been in "such a state of deterioration that it was risking their limbs to sit there on Sundays". He also said that the seats were very uncomfortable and had crashed to the floor on one occasion; the floor had given way and parts of the ceiling had begun to fall upon the worshippers. Money for the cost of renovation was raised by donations of a sovereign each from members, a sale of work and support from Mrs. Burgess and Mr. Hodge.

In the 1940s William Miller Higgs, who was compiling a history of the village, had noted that the Chapel which was Congregational in character was still affiliated to the Chapel in Goring under the Countess of Huntingdon's Connexion, and that the Minister of both Chapels was the Rev. S. H. Wing.

In 1961 an article in the Oxford Times, written by Peter Trickett about South Stoke, indicated that only some 40 chapels still remained within the Countess of Huntingdon's Connexion; and that *"the remainder have at one stage or another become affiliated with the*

Congregational Union of England and Wales, from whose ranks their Ministers are appointed". The article went on to say,

"*Among this number is South Stoke's Free Church, which nevertheless still takes pride in its old associations*".

At that time the minister of both Chapels was the Rev. Stuart Good. The South Stoke Chapel was closed down from 1948-54, but was then re-opened by the Rev. Edwin Thomas, with a membership of about 15 and a Sunday School of about the same number. Although congregation attendance remained constant and even increased in later years, the Chapel building itself was again in need of considerable repairs and renovations, for which funds were not available. Sadly, therefore in 1976 it was decided to close the Chapel.

The Chapel on the left in the early 1970s

The Goring Free Church now deliberated as to what could be done with the building and made various applications for planning permission to convert it to other uses, but these were all turned down. It then decided reluctantly to sell off the premises. The Parish Council became interested and put up proposals for conversion, but these too were rejected. And so, the old building stood empty and forlorn, but not forgotten, as by now a small new housing development had been completed opposite and had been aptly named Chapel Close.

When in 1982 Mr and Mrs Onians bought the Malt House property they decided at the same time to purchase the Chapel, which had been built on what was originally part of the Malt House property. This was agreed to on condition that the building should never be let out to any religious body for services of worship. The Onians then spent a considerable sum on basic remedial measures to prevent further deterioration of the old Chapel, whilst they considered to what purpose it should be put in the future.

The Chapel is today a listed building, described as of:

"*Red brick, with old plain-tile hipped roof. Single storey, single window range. Four panel door to centre with overlight. 9 paned horned sash above. Two 24 pane unhorned sashes to left return*". [1]

The Chapel today

The main entrance into the Chapel from the Street is at the east end of the building, where there was also an upstairs gallery. At the west end was the Minister's platform, with a lectern and behind this a door led into the adjacent Vestry room, where meetings, social events and Sunday schools were once held. On the front and sides of the Chapel initials can be seen, scratched into the brickwork, of those who helped with the building's construction and who later attended its Services.

The Chapel continued to be used for storage until July 2004, when new owners were eventually given planning permission to convert the Chapel into living accommodation for relatives. It still exists as a dwelling today (2020).

ENDNOTES:

1. Free Church--*"Buildings of England: Oxfordshire"* p.774 or britishlistedbuildings.co.uk .

Information regarding the Countess is courtesy of *"The Elect Lady, the Countess of Huntingdon (1707-1791)"* by G. W. Kirby published 1972.

The Malthouse Indenture 1821 regarding the South Stoke Chapel.

CHAPTER 5

HEALTH AND SOCIAL SERVICES IN SOUTH STOKE SINCE AD 1600

In 1601 the great Poor Relief Act of Elizabeth I was enacted, under which the Parish (the system of which dates from the Norman Conquest), through its executive body, the Vestry, became the local unit of administration for the poor. It had particular responsibility for looking after the old and disabled poor, pauper children and the able-bodied unemployed and also for handling rogues, vagabonds, strangers and destitutes. Overseers of the Poor were then appointed by the Vestry (which continued to deal with its usual ecclesiastical and civil matters) to carry out these specific duties in the parish. They were authorised to levy a poor rate on all householders, and to keep appropriate account books. These Overseers were henceforth to look after the poor and needy villagers from birth to death ensuring that such persons were adequately fed, clothed and housed. They paid for midwifery attention at birth, for old fashioned remedies to be provided at times of sickness or ill-health and, as a last resort, could call for such doctor as might be available. Finally, when death came, the poor could be assisted with funeral expenses.

The earliest account book of the Overseers of the Poor in the Parish of South Stoke-cum-Woodcote commences in 1702. Some early entries of poor relief indicate *"6d given to a traveller, 8d given to three sailors and 1/- to a woman big with child"*. During the following 80 years entries indicate regular payment to those in need, to persons *"when ill"* and when *"no work"*; and occasional entries of payments *"for going to the doctor"*. Epidemics however certainly required expert medical attention, and an entry for 1788 indicates that a doctor who was called for in connection with an outbreak of smallpox in the parish, was paid £12 by Woodcote and £3 by South Stoke. During 1795 and 1796 some typical entries were a payment to a Mrs Wilder *"for bleeding the poor 1/-* ", for the purchase of *"mutton and gin to Sarah Smith when ill 2/-* ", to Sarah Smith when *"her child arm broke 1/-*" and to *"Meria Smewin's children - ointment for itch 4/7d"*. Between 1815 and 1817 several payments were made to a leper.

The poor of South Stoke have also in the past received assistance from various charities set up by local benefactors and administered by the church wardens. The account books of such wardens indicate that in the 17th century charities were providing funds for *"greatcoats for men"*, for the schooling of local children and *for "flannel, calico, blankets and sheets for the poor"*. In the 18th century almshouses for the poor were set up and *"coal money"* was made available, which was augmented in the 19th century by a *"blanket money"* charity. As already mentioned old fashioned remedies were much used on the medical side, and were usually effective to deal with such minor ailments as sore throats, colds, coughs, earaches, bronchial ailments, constipation and diarrhoea. Children's ailments like measles, whooping cough, chickenpox or mumps were never taken very seriously. A doctor however was usually called in to deal with diphtheria, scarlet fever and pneumonia. In general, such serious illnesses were much dreaded, and a doctor in those days could only be found in Wallingford.

In 1834 the Poor Law Amendment Act laid down that no further poor relief should be given by parishes which, for such purposes, were then amalgamated into Unions. Thereafter the poor and needy of South Stoke had to be sent to the Wallingford Union Workhouse, where they were given work, shelter, food and very basic medical and nursing care. From 1851 onwards, there are frequent entries in South Stoke's burial register, showing *"the abode"* of a deceased villager as the Wallingford Union, the body then being brought back to the village for burial. Although responsibility for the poor had now been taken away from the Vestry, it continued to deal with other local matters until the 1894 Local Government Act set up new civil parishes throughout the country. Following this South Stoke's own Parish Council was established in 1899 and took over all responsibility for civil affairs, leaving the Vestry merely to deal with church matters.

Public health was never an issue of any particular importance in South Stoke; but two Public Health Acts were introduced in 1872 and 1875 which, regarding rural communities, gave the Poor Law Guardians considerable powers in such matters. As regards medical treatment in the country areas, doctors were still few and far between in those days and their services were costly. As a result they were generally beyond the reach of most villagers who were also in those times very sceptical of the medical 'quack'. As a result many went without medical care, turning instead to traditional remedies for illnesses and to patent medicines which were then in the 19th century becoming widely available. For childbirth no one looked beyond the village midwife or a kindly neighbour. In the hundred years after 1815 advancements in medical knowledge enabled doctors to overcome the popular scepticism of their abilities and to demonstrate their new skills. In 1858 the registration of doctors was made compulsory and in the same year the first school of nursing was set up at St Thomas' Hospital, London. Oxford already had its own hospital, the Radcliffe Infirmary, built in 1770 but now closed as adequate facilities exist in the modern John Radcliffe Hospital. Reading opened its Royal Berkshire Hospital in 1839, followed by Battle Hospital and the Fairmile Mental Hospital at Cholsey.

The granting of the first old age pension in 1908 was a great help for the elderly. The 1911 National Insurance Act was also of considerable assistance to the lower paid workers, who now for a small contribution of 4d a week received free medical attention and a payment of 10/- a week when they fell ill. Health services for the poor however remained the responsibility of the Poor Law Unions until 1929, when a Local Government Act abolished these Unions and transferred their duties and buildings to the new County and County Borough Councils, which had been set up in 1888. These now assumed responsibilities for maternal/child/health, midwives, ambulances, health centres and home nursing. Although South Stoke was later to come under Goring for these services, initially it came under Wallingford, where the old workhouse was now rebuilt as St Mary's Hospital (since demolished) and where St George's Maternity Hospital was also built (since incorporated into the school). Local authorities now began to show a much greater interest in the health and welfare of their local people.

At the end of the Great War, Lloyd George announced that the land would now be made *"fit for heroes to live in"*, but in fact the post war economic difficulties led to a major recession and his resignation as Prime Minster in 1922. In those years between the wars private medical insurance schemes (in addition to the national scheme) became popular and were much used by those in South Stoke. Mrs Jessie Bullock, the wife of a local farmer, was prominent in those days in assisting to advise on and collect contributions to a scheme organised by the Royal Berkshire Hospital. The hospital was a good one but when in 1937 it experienced financial difficulties, many rural villages in its area including South Stoke raised funds through fetes, dances and similar activities to help out. During World War II the Beveridge Report of 1942 became the blueprint for the great increase in social services that was to follow the end of the war.

On 5th July 1948, the National Health Service was inaugurated *"to promote the establishment of a comprehensive Health Service, designed to secure improvement in the mental and physical health of the people of England and Wales (a separate service was set up for Scotland and Northern Ireland) and the prevention, diagnosis and treatment of illness"*. The new NHS now covered a comprehensive range of hospital, specialist medical, dental, ophthalmic practitioner services for every man, woman and child in the country. Patients could be treated in the surgery or at home, and doctors could prescribe all drugs and medicines necessary for their patients. At the same time the National Insurance and Assistance Scheme came into operation, providing for a wide range of benefits, including sickness, maternity and unemployment. These were eligible for all, following payments of contributions by employed persons and employers alike. Since then the NHS has had numerous structural and managerial changes and increased demand and budget shortfalls continue to create problems.

There has never been a practising doctor or qualified midwife with surgery facilities in South Stoke. However there is the well-known story of a remarkable woman, who lived in the village *"many many years ago"* and who served as midwife to the local families. In those days ante-natal and obstetric care were virtually unknown, and childbirth could be a dangerous business, resulting in high maternal and infant mortality. However the woman in question devoted most of her life to acting as the unqualified, though experienced and highly successful midwife to the mothers of the village. In her youth she had been happily married to a young man and they lived in a small cottage by one of the railway arches. Unfortunately her husband then stole a sheep, the carcass of which was discovered under the floor of their house. He was arrested, tried and convicted; and allegedly transported. His young wife was left to live out her life in South Stoke, ever faithful to her lost husband, but who now devoted herself to practising as the village midwife. She grew to become the loved *"Granny"* of the many children she so successfully brought into the world. Whilst she never forgot her husband, her life was made joyful by her *"many children"*.

In the 1860s a number of new Victorian brick cottages were built in South Stoke for the local farm workers, in addition to two earlier cottages for railway supervisors. As part of the overall plan to improve the general public health situation throughout the country, the Artisans Dwelling Act of 1875 was a first step in enabling local authorities to clear city slums, and to embark on housing schemes *"with special regard to the accommodation of the working classes"*. After the Great War, housing for the poorer population still remained a major problem; and the newly created Ministry of Health in 1919 introduced a Housing Act to improve the situation, with subsidies being given to local authorities to build the houses that were required. This led to new housing estates being built in the1920s along the Wallingford Road (B4009).

These enabled the occupants of the old and unhygienic thatched cottages at the south west end of the village to move out and occupy the new houses, leaving the old cottages to be demolished in the 1920s (see next page).

All these houses including a farmhouse were demolished in the 1920s

Glebe Cottages on the corner of South Bank and the Wallingford Road

A few years later a further 10 such houses were built on glebe land to the west of Wallingford Road; with every pair of houses having its own water handpump. In 1930, 8 more council houses were built down Cross Keys Road. By then mains water had come to the village. After World War II, 12 more such council houses were erected on South Bank Road.

As regards life in the village in the early 1900s, cottages were always available for the married families, with their own wells and outside privvies. Though poor, the people were happy and had no regrets about their way of life. The village was an agricultural community, very self-contained, with plenty of work for the men on the various farms and in their associated trades; with families able to buy all they needed in the various village shops. A local school catered for the needs of the children, and kept them busy from the age of 3 up to about 14. After school there were plenty of other occupations or pleasures for them to follow. The poorest families ate bread and lard, sprinkled with brown sugar; but most were able to produce a hot meal every day, cooked in a big black pot hung over an open fire: into this would usually go all three courses, each in its own cooking bag, meat in one, the vegetables in another and a pudding in the third - all cooked together. Many families kept pigs, which went into the main meals and produced home-made bacon. Corn, eggs and dairy products were plentiful: whilst the fruits and berries of the countryside provided jams and jellies. Dinner was normally at 11 am, with supper at 5 or 6 pm. Snacks could be taken in between, whilst ales and cakes could be consumed at any time. Farm workers normally carried their midday meal with them into the fields. Life was hard, but was a happy and healthy one.

In the early years of the 20th century a Dr. Nelson used to be the parish doctor, who rode over from Wallingford to visit the sick poor people of the village. Thereafter South Stoke came under Goring, and a doctor of more recent years (between the wars) who is remembered in the village with great affection was Dr. Bourdillon of Goring. A particular memory of him relates to the very hard winter of 1937, when he was required to visit one of his patients in South Stoke. As the roads were impassable due to deep snow drifts, he came over by horse-drawn sledge through the fields. He serviced the Goring community equally well, and on his death the Bourdillon sports field, behind the primary school at Cleeve, was acquired by public subscription and dedicated to his memory. Dr. Beet then took over his practice. Dr. Evans of Stow House in Goring, and his partner Dr. Leslie of Streatley, were also much loved practitioners. Both doctors used to cycle over to South Stoke from Goring where they helped many poor families. Dr. Monk of Goring, who had earlier been a young assistant to Dr. Bourdillon, now joined the practice and worked with Dr. Thomas of Streatley, who had married Dr. Leslie's daughter. Dr. Dixie of Streatley was also active in the area, and was in addition a heart specialist.

Over the years there have been a smattering of doctors and medical workers in the village but only living here as residents, either retired or working elsewhere. However in April of 1981 Goring acquired the Red Cross Road Surgery, built at the instigation of Drs. Monk and Dixie. This now forms part of the Goring and Woodcote Medical Practice. Both surgeries provide the medical help to the villagers of South Stoke.

The Higgs' Memorial on the north wall of the chancel, St Andrew's Church

CHAPTER 6

THE SOUTH STOKE CHARITIES

Following on from the Health and Social Services chapter, it is interesting to note that worthies from as long ago as the early 1600s showed concern for those less well off than themselves in this particular parish.These unfortunates had no government "safety net" to protect them. Today the charity funds have dwindled into an irrelevance but in their day no doubt the money and clothing was much appreciated.

A note by Rev. Philip Nind, in the South Stoke churchwardens' accounts for 1863-1893 records that the Waistcoat Money Charity was made available by one Augustine Knapp in 1602, only a year after Elizabeth I's Poor Relief Act. He charged his Paradise Estate near Henley with the payment of 20/- a year towards clothing for the *"poor, lame, impotent and needy people"* of this parish. It has always been called the Waistcoat Money, but for many years had been distributed (every three years) in *"warm clothing"*. In 1881 the rent charge was redeemed for £34 stock yielding 16s 8d. The value over the years has diminished to 10/- being given in clothing vouchers to one person in South Stoke and one in Woodcote in the 1950s. Since then two people (from Woodcote and South Stoke) received a small sum annually but the charity now no longer exists having been amalgamated with another.

In 1659 Dr. Griffith Higgs' executors were directed that from part of his estate £100 should be given to the church *"to buy land for ye poore*". It seems that an island in the Thames, of about one and a half acres and rich in osier beds, was originally bought (together with a small plot of land north of the railway line and Ferry Road) and duly let out for rent; from the proceeds of which the executors were charged to set aside £5 annually for the poor of the parish. Philip Nind, who took a great interest in these matters, has left a note in the register of burials for 1813-1903 concerning this charity, which reads *"£5 a year to the poor of South Stoke, to be divided as follows; £3 to be distributed yearly among six poor families of South Stoke below hill,* (that is the village of South Stoke itself) *and £2 to six poor families of Woodcote, by half yearly payments at Christmas and Easter in each year. The money is procured from an acre and a quarter of meadow at South Stoke called the Doctor's Gift*".

The sale of these pieces of land was authorised in 1948, when the proceeds were invested in £334 stock.[1] The trustees were the vicar and a churchwarden or person nominated by the vicar. They then determine who receives the money. Another legacy from the Higgs' estate was money for education. By the early decades of the 20th century the charity is referred to as the South Stoke Educational Charity or the South Stoke Free School Charity in the school log book. In 1915 eighteen children received 10/- each from the charity but by 1924 the *"gift"* had become boots and clothing rather than cash and the recipients numbered twelve. Recipients fluctuated over the years being as low as three in 1932.[2] In 2020 the charity has evolved into supporting students (living in South Stoke or Woodcote) as they progress through the state system of education. Land had been purchased in Woodcote known as School Piece. This was rented out and together with money invested with the Charity Commissioners and a sizeable donation from a local event there is a goodly amount to disperse. In 2019 awards were presented to 21 students totalling £1,735. Book tokens worth £25 and £35 were presented to primary and secondary students who went on to further education from Langtree School in Woodcote. Cheques of £50-£60 were also presented to 1st,2nd and 3rd year further education students. Currently, there are four trustees represented by South Stoke church, Woodcote parish council, Oxfordshire County Council and a representative from the University of Reading.[3]

A note in the burial register, written again by Rev. Nind, sets out the details of The Greatcoat Charity. This indicates that "*Henry Parslow (of Woodcote) in 1675, charged his estate, of Roomer Edge (or Rumer Hedge) in the parish of Checkendon, with the payment of £5 to provide five coats for five poor men, one at South Stoke, two at Woodcote and two at Checkendon*". Parslow also directed that the vicar of South Stoke should receive 10/-, for preaching a sermon on the Monday before All Saints Day; the clerk 1/- and the two churchwardens who were to buy the coats 1/- each. In 1937 the rent charge was redeemed for £260 stock, and the income therefrom provided for a small sum of money to be given annually to the five selected men from the three villages, with which to buy a greatcoat. In 1872 only three coats were provided and this dwindled so that in 1943 the five poor men of the three villages would receive 30/- apiece. If five poor could not be found the money was rolled over so that in 1957 it was worth £3.

Another charity, arising out of a £40 gift made by an unknown donor before 1786, together with income from another anonymous benefactor of land on which two cottages in South Stoke once stood (they were given in 1877, but were burnt down in the fire of 1905), provided about £6 in the 1950s.This was to be paid to some eight or nine recipients in South Stoke and Woodcote for the purchase of coal.

Today (2020) there is what is known as The Fuel Charity for the poor and needy of South Stoke only. Payments are distributed approximately every 3 years.

A fifth charity is that known as the Blanket Money, some details of which are outlined in the churchwardens' accounts for 1863-1893. It arises from a legacy of Mrs Jane Williams of Bourton on the Hill, Gloucestershire. Her will, which was proved in 1831, provided for £100 in 3% stock, the interest of which was to be used for the benefit of the poor in South Stoke and Chastleton parishes. Since 1833 this charity has paid out equal amounts for South Stoke and Woodcote, to enable needy persons to purchase blankets. By the 1950s the income was £2 10s 0d yearly distributed in clothing vouchers to the value of 10/-. It permits that four persons annually to receive around £1 each. This charity still exists today but distribution occurs possibly every 2-3 years now and the amount can vary. The criteria is still for the poor and needy but only in South Stoke.

There are two other charities relating to Woodcote only. (When the parish of South Stoke is considered it has to be remembered that until 1952 Woodcote was part of the South Stoke-cum-Woodcote parish). One is the endowment by Susannah Newman, who died in 1715, to establish a school at Woodcote. The other is the bequest by William Claxson, whose will (proved in 1860) left £291 stock to buy clothing for the poor of Woodcote. There were once two other charities for the parish which since have lapsed.

Meanwhile, South Stoke still has a right to benefit from Allnutt's Almshouse at Goring Heath by sending one poor man there and certainly in the 19th century *"a certain number of poor boys ...... (could) participate in the benefits"* this charity had to offer. There is only one entry in the early 20th century school log book of this Goring Heath charity. In April of 1925 a boy and a girl were to receive money *"in lieu of apprenticeships"*.[4]

ENDNOTES:

1.The Victoria County History – Oxfordshire -South Stoke. There is a section on the Charities of South Stoke.

2. South Stoke School Log Book 1913-1942

3. Dr Higgs' Educational Trust report for the South Stoke Annual Parish Meeting 2019

4. South Stoke School Log Book 1913-1942-April 1925

The Hannes' Memorial commemorating Richard Hannes, Lord of the Manor in the mid-17th century and his wife Jane. Situated on the east wall of the chancel, St Andrew's Church

CHAPTER 7

LORDS OF THE MANOR

Immediately on the north side of the church is the site of Manor Farm. Originally, Eynsham Abbey's manor house was located here and was known to have existed in the mid 14th century. As early as the 16th century the farm was known as Barre Place and the "horizontal" road running alongside the site in the foreground was known as Barreway (now Ferry Road). The large upright building in the centre of the photo is the listed dovecote which housed 1500 nest boxes around its walls. The farmhouse itself probably dates from the 16th century with later extensions being added throughout the centuries.

In medieval times the basis of wealth was the ownership of land, much of which was owned by the church. The landowners in South Stoke were initially the Bishops of Dorchester, later transferring to the bishopric of Lincoln in about 1080 and then passing to the Abbots of Eynsham from 1094. The abbot was responsible for appointing the incumbents and imposing tithes, and later for leasing the land with the title. The lessees of the manor were known as Lords of the Manor. They or their steward held manorial courts which played an important part in the life of the parish.

Records are inadequate until 1460 when Eynsham Abbey leased both farm and manor to Henry Doget and John Felowe (both officials of the Abbot). They were followed in 1476 by Geoffrey and Morgan Kydewelly, who were "*two of the many Welshmen to hold office in the county*" at that time. However, neither the Welshmen nor the Abbot's officials were resident in South Stoke being absentee landlords. The next Lord of the Manor was to be Walter Barton, from Herefordshire, who acquired the lease in 1536. He left it on his death a year later (since he had no issue) to his nephew Griffith Barton, who was the first member of that family to live at South Stoke.

1546 saw a major change of ownership in the parish when all the land in South Stoke, previously held by Eynsham Abbey was given over to Christ Church in Oxford at the command of Henry VIII. However, the College continued the Abbey's previous practice of leasing out both land and manor. When Griffith Barton died in 1579 the lease of the manor and its land passed to one of his six daughters, Margaret, and to her husband William Palmer, who was auditor of Christ Church. William died in 1598, leaving the lease to his son Barton Palmer.

As the Victoria County History has indicated, Barton Palmer "*had no sons*" and so, before his death in about 1605, *"for the advancement and maintenance"* of his wife, Mary and his two daughters, he granted the lease of Stoke for a term of years to Hugh Keate of Hagbourne (Oxfordshire, formerly in Berkshire), a relative. In 1610 the lease of forty years seems to have passed to Mary Palmer's second husband Henry Arden. When he died in 1622 the manor probably went to Edward Wollascott, whose father had married one of Barton Palmer's two daughters.

By 1642 the manor had passed to Richard Hannes (1596-1678) the son of an Oxford brewer, (see page 78). For some reason (see next memorial image), in 1657 Richard's son-in-law William Barber of Adderbury appeared to be holding the manorial courts. However by 1689 it was William Barber's son Robert *"on whose wife the lease of Stoke had been settled on her marriage"* who took on the lease which, on his death in 1714, passed in turn to his son Edward Barber.

In 1719 Kemp Harward, a physician of London[1] became Lord of the Manor and was to surrender his lease in 1740 to his daughter Lucy, a spinster at this time of Bourton-on-the-Hill, Gloucestershire.[2] However, by 1747 she had married John Head and for some years the lease was administered by trustees of the marriage settlement (John Dewes and Richard Southby)[3] until John Head, now in Hodcot, Berkshire, began to take over in 1769.[4] (See memorial below, page 84).

The Rev. Thomas Williams, Rector of Beer-Regis, Dorset, took over the Lordship in 1803,[5] after which the manor passed to a Non-Conformist, Isaac King. He had begun renting Manor Farm in 1819 but only formally took over the lease in 1831.[6] Surprisingly King was instrumental in the formation of a Dissenting Chapel in the

Unfinished memorial of Mrs. William Barber on the east wall of the chancel

village but Christ Church did not appear to be concerned. He was the last of the Lords of the Manor, for in 1860 Christ Church ceased to lease out the manorial rights and title though it continued to rent out the house and farmland.[7] The land is still leased to the Bullock family (2020) who have worked the farm since the nineteenth century but the farmhouse itself was sold off in 1998.

ENDNOTES:

1. Oxon.South Stoke A 14-15 17 Dec. 1719 Christ Church Archives.

2. Oxon.South Stoke A 21-22 31 Oct. 1740 Christ Church Archives.

3. Oxon.South Stoke A 23 16 Nov.1747 Christ Church Archives.

4. Oxon.South Stoke A 26 9 Jan. 1769 Christ Church Archives.

5. Oxon. South Stoke A 34-35 10 Dec. 1803 Christ Church Archives.

6. Oxon. South Stoke A 40 14 Dec 1831 Christ Church Archives.

7. All the information otherwise is found in The Victoria County History-Oxfordshire- South Stoke-Manor.

Early 20th century image taken from the north of the site of Manor Farm showing from left to right, the dovecote, the granary on staddle stones and the farmhouse

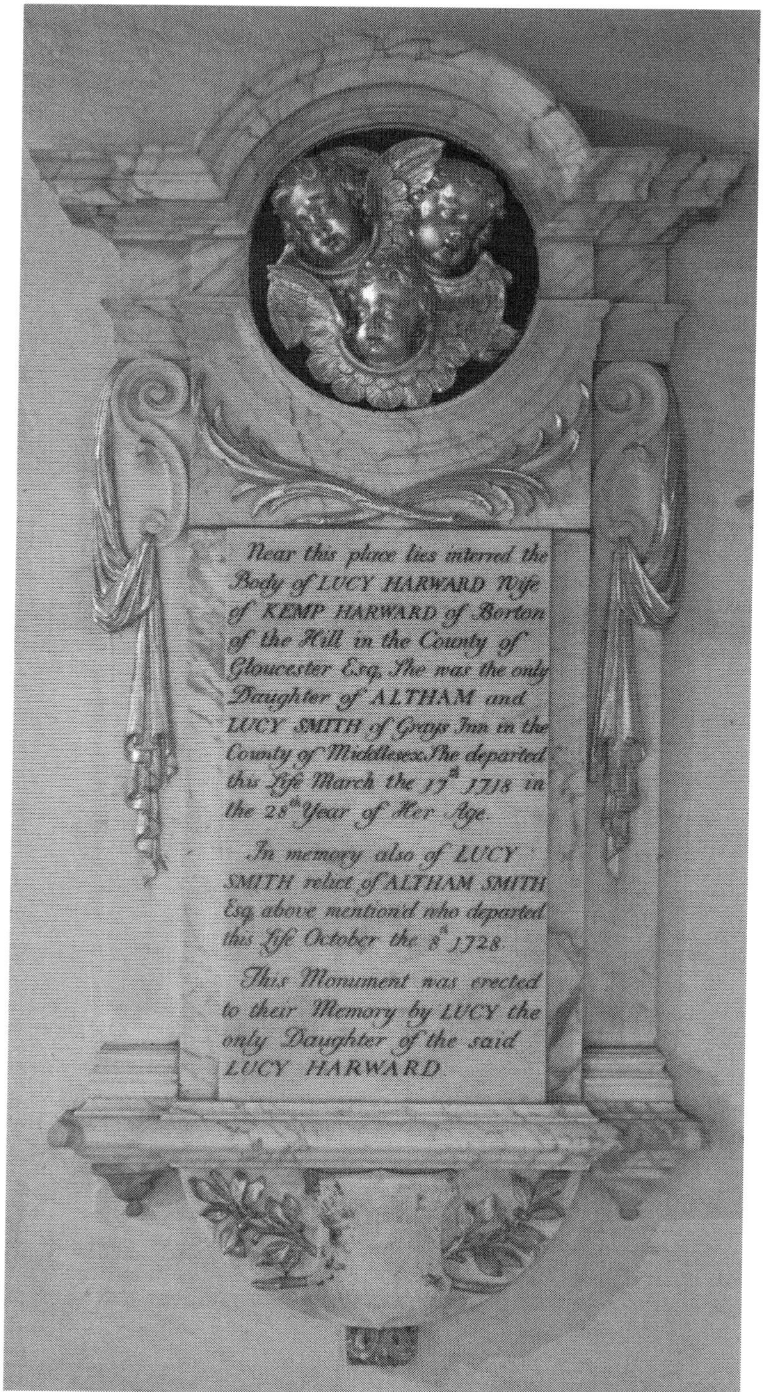

The Harward Memorial on the north wall of the chancel of St Andrew's Church

CHAPTER 8

AGRICULTURE AND FARMING IN SOUTH STOKE CUM WOODCOTE

Before the 10th century the land around South Stoke was originally in the control of the Saxon Bishop of Dorchester, but by 1086 the seat of the bishopric had been moved northwards to Lincoln and South Stoke remained for a time under that bishop's control.

The Domesday Survey of 1086 indicated that this estate of *"STOCH"* [1] comprised some 24 acres of meadow land. The bishop held seventeen *"hides"* and one *"virgate"* of land equalling approximately 2,065 acres. Of this acreage 960 acres (8 hides) were *"in demesne"*. That is, land kept by the Lord (Bishop) himself or farmed for his own profit. The remaining acreage of 1,105 was in the hands of nineteen *"villeins"*; those unfree peasants who owed labour (2-3 days a week) to their Lord but who also farmed land for themselves. Five *"bordars"* also held parcels of land under similar conditions to the villeins though of less acreage. Then there was one unfortunate *"serf"* who had no land whatsoever.[2]

In 1094, South Stoke was assigned by the Bishop of Lincoln to Eynsham Abbey (a transfer that was confirmed by Henry I in 1109), which continued to run the demesne farm. This and the rest of the estate was run under a two field system of strip holdings, but by 1279 when some thirty two peasant tenant holders were working the land, the old open two field system had given way to three large open fields - the South, Middle and North - with two being cropped in rotation and the third lying fallow. The fields were all unhedged but some of the old acre strips had now been amalgamated into slightly larger strips. David Hall writing in *"The Open Fields of England"* states that the change from two to three field systems occurred in South Stoke between 1240 and 1350.[3] About 1220-1227 there is mention of a windmill belonging to the Manor where the Abbey's villein tenants were obliged to grind their corn. The crops grown in the 13th century were wheat, mixtillia (a wheat and rye mixture), barley, corn cut green (tramasium) and oats.

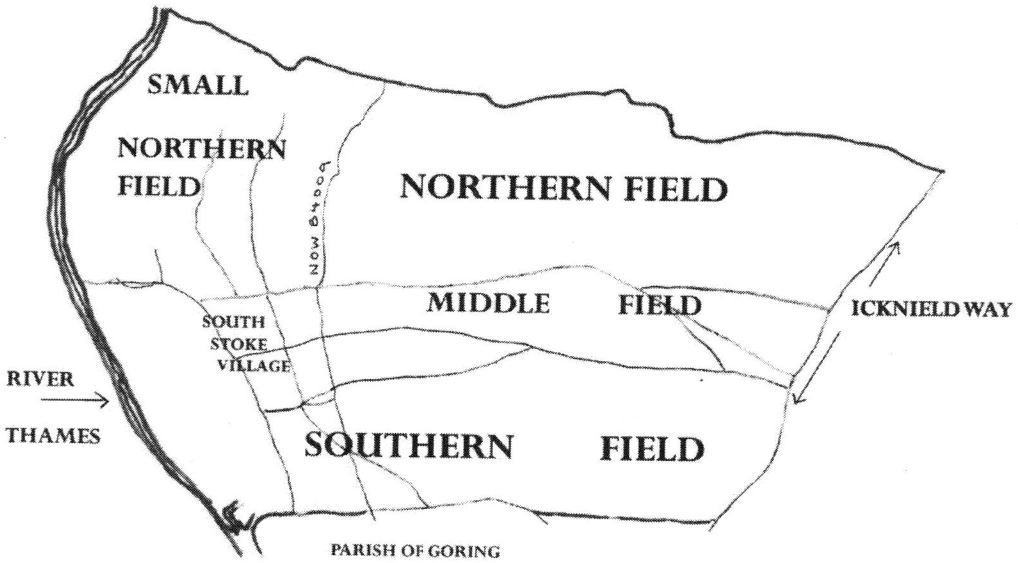

Map based upon the information from the Eynsham Cartulary Vol. II showing the field layout c.1366 in the western section of the parish of South Stoke cum Woodcote.

Throughout the 14th century all had obligations to do service to the abbey in some form or other. The villeins particularly had to do their share in all farming activities on the demesne land throughout the calendar year as farming was still predominantly arable.

In 1460 Eynsham Abbey ceased running its own demesne farm and instead began to lease out both its farm and the title of the Lord of the Manor. (A manor is an administrative unit of a landed estate which can vary in acreage and may cover one or more parishes. Tenants paid rent or service, had to abide by the customs and courts of the manor and even succeeded to their land only through the manorial courts). Arable farming continued on most of the land growing wheat, barley, corn and oats with some pasture land being set aside for sheep rearing. By 1530 the number of tenants had declined to seventeen or eighteen, but with most having a much greater holding than before of around 60 acres. Thereafter, with the decline of the feudal system, the villein peasant was to become ever more emancipated and, as a yeoman farmer, was increasingly to take more responsibility for the use of his land (though still as tenant to the landowner).

1546 saw a major change of ownership when all land in South Stoke was removed from Eynsham Abbey by order of Henry VIII and given over to Christ Church in Oxford. However, the 16th and 17th centuries produced *"many prosperous yeoman families"* with the general population beginning to grow quite rapidly.

By 1665 the parish of South Stoke had some 33 houses assessed for the Hearth Tax (where each liable householder had to pay 1/- twice a year for every fire, stove or hearth in the property). The 17th and 18th centuries saw several small and medium sized farms in existence, apart from the main Manor farm which by 1740 comprised some 350-400 acres of open-field land, still in strips of a few acres. In addition, fifteen individual tenant farms (four with holdings of over 50 acres), consisted of strips of land spread over the riverside meadows and the three unhedged open fields - now known as Great North (north of the Barreway), Great South and Little North (north west of the village) - amounting to some 1000 acres. An early agricultural map of 1818 shows clearly the strip field layout of South Stoke at that time.[4]

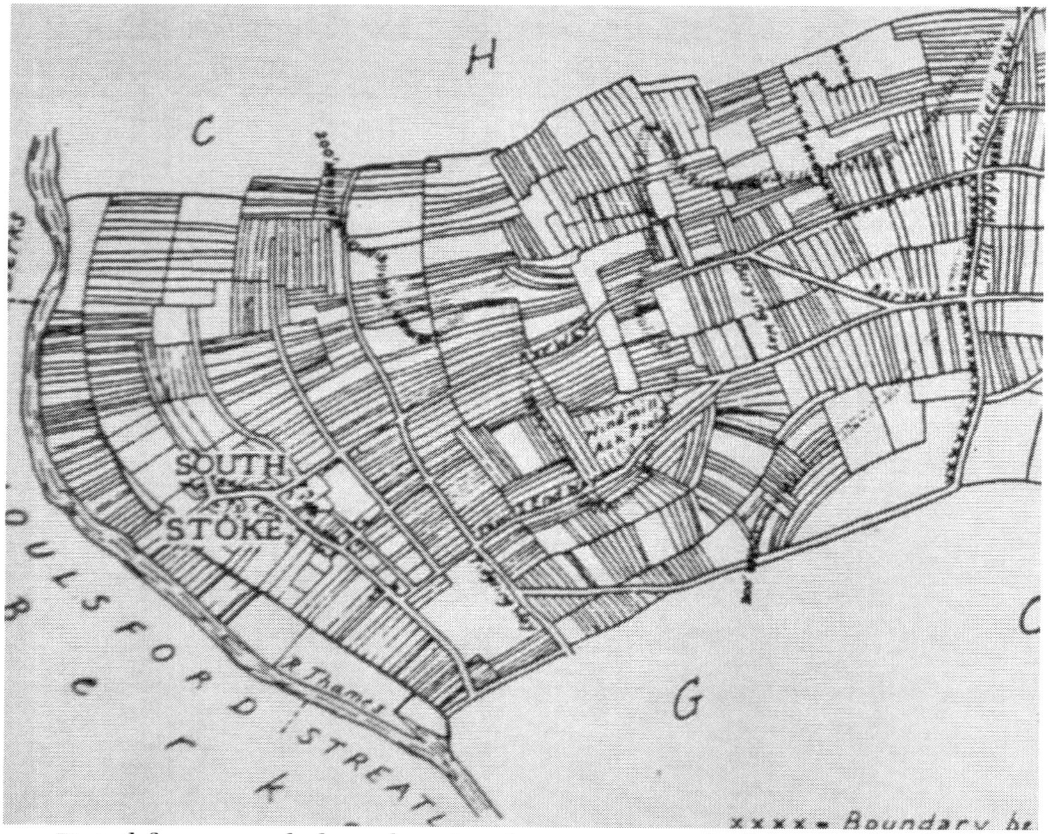

Detail from map below showing the western end of the parish of South Stoke in 1818 before the railway and enclosures

By 1819, Manor Farm had some 314 acres. For a short time College Farm exceeded Manor Farm in size, with Arthur Spokes the lessee gradually acquiring from Christ Church the leases to other farms in the village. However, the 19th century still saw the parish as one consisting of numerous farms. There were the Panters, Fulbrooks, Waseys, Woodwards, Suttons, Spearinks, Kings, Butlers, Pithers, Brocks, Clares, Stevens and Vickerys. Their farms included Kaffirs, Icknield, Lower Farm, Waises, Corner House Farm, Brocks, Vickerys, Fulbrooks, the Malthouse, Ivy House Farm, Ivol Barn, and Lower Cadleys. However, in the latter part of the century and into the 20th century Christ Church incorporated many of these smaller farms into its Manor Farm.

In 1836, the great Tithe Act had been passed, which was to authorise the commuting of church tithes (previously payable in kind) to a cash rental charge, based on prices of wheat, barley and oats produced on local landholdings. For centuries tithes had been assessed as a tenth of all agricultural/animal produce and been a constant source of irritation to all concerned. It had led to incessant friction between vicar and farmer generally and from about 1815 with a series of vicars completely absent from the village this had certainly caused grumblings in South Stoke. From the 17th century onwards various agricultural reformists had advocated the abolition of tithes in kind, on the grounds that it created many difficulties for farmers and militated against changes in agricultural practice. Quakers refused absolutely to pay tithes as being unchristian! In South Stoke the payments of tithes in kind became a cash rental charge in 1846, when a tithe map setting out all agricultural land holdings was produced, together with accompanying schedules of respective land holders.

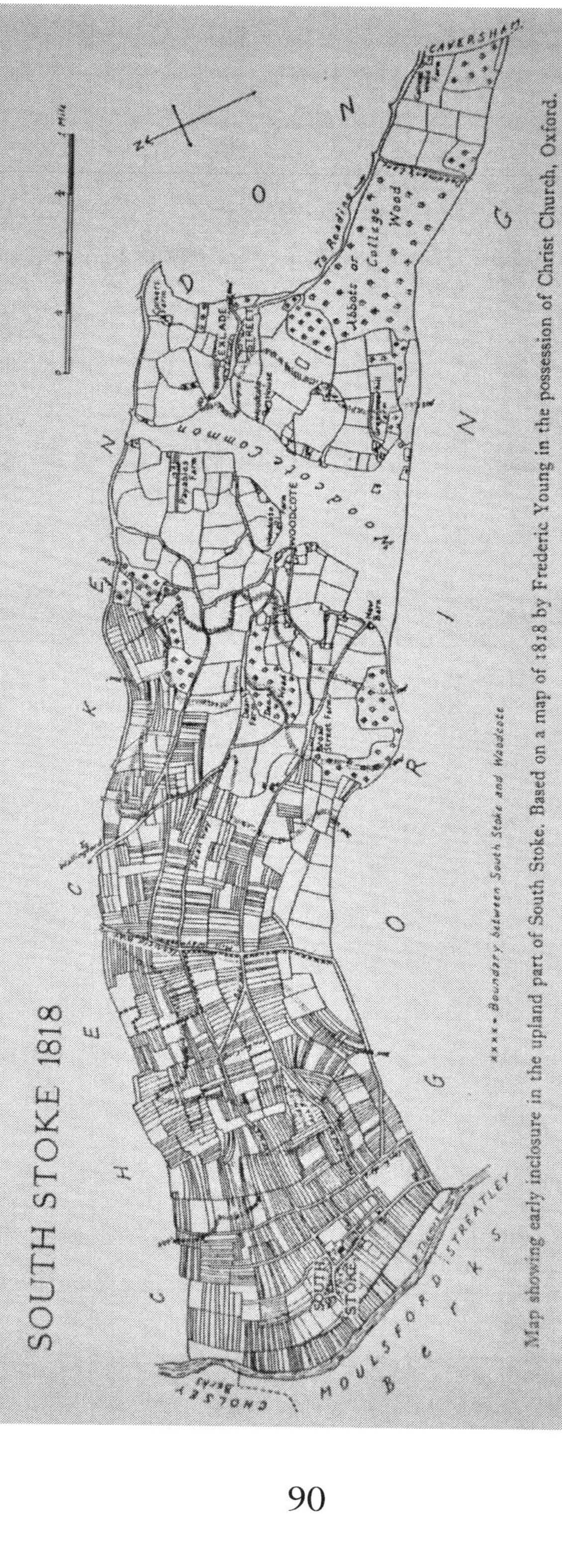

Map showing early inclosure in the upland part of South Stoke. Based on a map of 1818 by Frederic Young in the possession of Christ Church, Oxford.

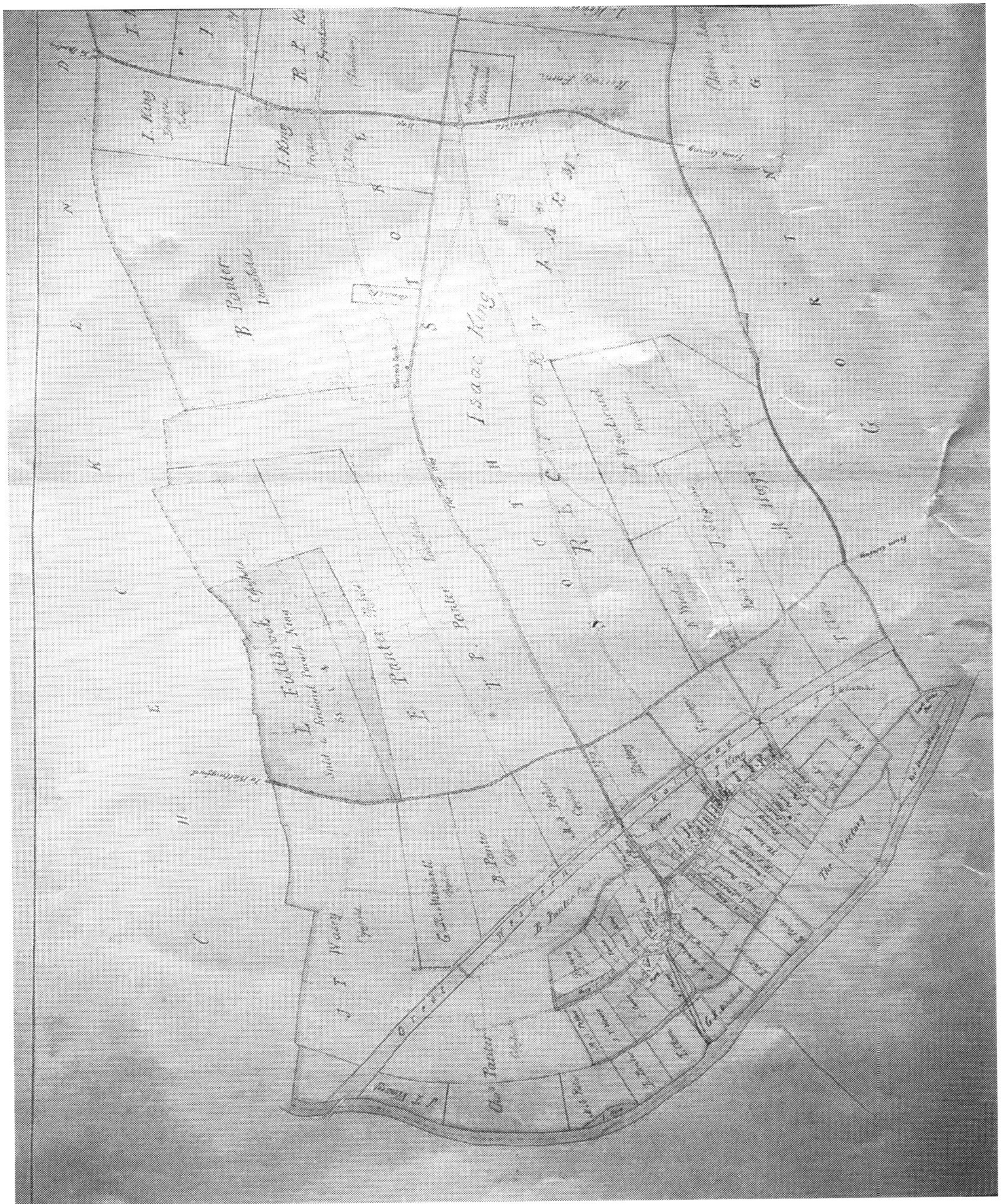

The 1855 Badcock map above. The earlier 1818 map of South Stoke shows the strip farming in the west of the parish pre-enclosure but by 1855 this map shows the larger field system post-enclosure.

This indicated a total cash tithe for the parish of South Stoke-cum-Woodcote of £892, of which £765 was to go to Christ Church and £127 to the Vicar.[5] The information thus set out was of great value to those who produced the Enclosure Award of 1853. And that Award in turn prompted the production of a fresh tithe map in September of that year.

The Enclosure Award of 1853 enclosed some 1750 acres of land in South Stoke. It was to have a dramatic effect on agriculture in general, since it was to change the open field strip system of cultivation into individual registered holdings, amalgamated into separate, hedged fields. All land so recorded was awarded to tenants as either freehold or copyhold (the former giving the greater security and the latter less so, since after three generations the tenant had to pay a substantial sum to renew the lease). This arrangement was ultimately to serve as title deeds.

Although some of the smaller farmers experienced problems Christ Church, Manor Farm and the local vicar co-operated in alleviating the changes and difficulties, so that there was no real distress in the village. By 1870, it was thought the village must have been largely self-supporting. Beside the ten to fourteen farms which supplied most of the essential food, there was a butcher and a baker who also sold groceries, a tailor and shoemaker, two carpenters, blacksmiths and wheel wrights. There were three public houses and many farms brewed and sold beer to refresh thirsty farm labourers.

Isaac King, as the lessee of Manor Farm, was allotted about 260 acres; with a further 145 acres outside that farm in his own right. The next largest land allocation went to the Panter and Fulbrook families with Benjamin Panter alone receiving over 149 acres, John and Mary Wasey received 61 acres, Richard Woodward 45 and Martha Higgs 36. Cyrus Pether gained about 18 acres and the Vicar had 20 acres of glebe land in two fields (on either side of the present South Bank Road and east of the railway). The Trustees of the Free School gained 19 acres (in one field, still known by that name, off the Woodcote Road), William Stevens received 18 acres and Richard Pocock King 15. The remaining acreage went to some 14 minor land holders.[6] A major change arising out of these enclosures was that a number of the old roads or tracks that had previously existed were now incorporated into enclosed fields and hence ceased to exist. Some alteration to the landscape had also occurred with the building of the Great Western Railway in 1838-40 passing to the east of the village.

For the next 100 years after 1853 South Stoke remained essentially an agricultural community of farmers, labourers and the associated trades that went with it. All of its farms in the west of the parish had been situated in the village itself but once the enclosure took place Icknield Farm and Lower Cadleys were built outside the settlement near the Icknield Way close to the land being worked. In the census of 1871 although there were only six farmers listed in the village, they provided employment for 63 agricultural workers, 5 shepherds, and 12 farmers' boys.

In 1860 Christ Church ceased to lease out the manorial rights of its estate, though it continued to rent the Manor Farm. These rights had together with the farm been leased out since 1460 by first Eynsham Abbey and then Christ Church. Thus Isaac King was to be the last of a long line of Lords of the Manor in South Stoke. He, and then, his family continued to lease Manor Farm until 1870 when the brothers George and John Bullock took over the lease adding it to their existing College Farm holding, giving them a total of some 700 acres of good farm land.

The brothers John and George Bullock c.1913

An inventory of the College Farm in 1873 shows that the farm was then keeping 9 horses, 84 sheep, 86 lambs, 8 rams, 2 sows, 87 hogs, 29 store pigs, 10 fowls and 4 geese. It had wheat valued at £515-2-0, barley £424-4-0, oats £70-4-0, peas £33-5-0, beans £35-0-0, hay £150-0-0, clover seed £19-0-0 and turnips £46-10-0. There were also wagons, ploughs, harrows, rollers, drills and various other implements valued at £254-10-0. College Farm at this time employed 12 men at weekly wages of 20/- for a head carter, 15/- for an undercarter, 14/- for ploughmen, 13/- for shepherds and

12/- for labourers. At Manor Farm 20 men were employed at similar wages.[7]

Mrs Morgan at College Farm fronting Ferry Lane, in the early 20th century

The Bullock brothers on amalgamating the two farms set about getting all the land into full production. They established a large flock of sheep on the pasture land and soon had all the arable land under cultivation. They quickly built a reputation for efficient agricultural methods and for being good employers.

It would seem that by now there were virtually no hedges in existence around the fields, the boundaries around which were all well known to the local farmers. The appearance of the land was therefore very much as it is today (2020).

There were many difficulties in the 1870s and 1880s. First there was a series of wet seasons, with an especially bad summer in 1879. There were poor crops and much animal disease. The next problem was a flood of cheap corn, meat and wool into England from the New World and the Dominions. The price of wheat in 1877 had averaged 56/9d per quarter, by 1881 it had fallen to 31/-, and by 1894 to 20/- a quarter, and this led to cutbacks in the wheat acreage throughout the country. The price of wool was also falling alarmingly. So there were many problems facing farmers in those days, a situation which was not to improve until 1914. Nonetheless both the farm and the local community appeared to survive these difficulties.[8] In 1914 70% of agricultural land was arable and 29% pasture according to The Victoria County History.

Boys began work on the farms at any age between ten and fifteen. A boy's wages was around two shillings and sixpence (nearly 13p) a week, of which he would be expected to give at least two shillings to his mother for his keep. An adult worker in around 1900 earned between 9 and 13 shillings (45 to 65p) a week, a carter might earn 11 shillings plus a rent free tied cottage and a skilled shepherd 13 shillings. Other skilled workers such as thatchers might earn twice a shepherd's wage.

"The money was alright for ordinary living" it was maintained, *"but when it came to buying a pair of shoes it was very hard to manage".*

Memories from The Happy Circle Book recall that *"at harvest time many women went out into the fields with their children gleaning. The large families were able to pick up enough corn to last them throughout the winter, the corn being taken to a friendly miller to be ground into flour".* After the harvest there was *"Michaelmas Money"* which often amounted to more than five pounds. Wages may have reached 15 shillings a week by the time The Great War broke out and a farm worker who joined the army in 1914 was granted by the government 19 shillings a week as "separation money"- to maintain a wife and two children.[9] Allotments proved a popular way to help provide vegetables for the table and many families kept pigs and poultry. Fish, rabbits, rooks, larks and even sparrows were eaten regularly, so that there was no real malnutrition. The Bullock brothers took a keen interest in the local community and its affairs. John, who never married, became a churchwarden in 1874 and held the post for 41 years: he and George were both members of the School Committee. George, who married Mary, became a Parish Councillor, District Councillor, an Overseer of the Poor and a churchwarden at various times. His first three children, Harry, George and Frank were all born at College Farm and after 1878 five further children were born at their home in Manor Farm.

Manor Farm from the embankment with Ferry Road on the right in 1931

The youngest son, William took over the tenancy of Manor Farm following the death of his father George in 1925 (John had died earlier in 1916.) He sold off the sheep and brought in Irish cattle. There were then 22 cart horses working on the farm. Twelve to fourteen men were employed, and despite the hard times William maintained their wages at 30/- per week although at other farms they had fallen to 28/- or less. In 1930 William acquired his first tractor, and the horses were gradually phased out, the last horse leaving the farm in 1950. The farm just survived the Depression, and by 1933 a recovery had started and a period of prosperity began at the farm. In 1935 Eric Small joined his father at the farm, eventually becoming foreman in 1952 and continuing to work there until his retirement in 1993. From 1930 onwards the mechanization of the farm proceeded apace with the result that it became economical to enlarge many of the farm's fields east of the village; and thus any remaining hedges saw their removal being accelerated by the needs of food production during World War II.

William Bullock died in 1952 and the lease of Manor Farm was taken over by his son Frank. By this time the whole farm was mechanised, and entirely devoted to arable production. There were more than 500 acres of high quality malting barley being grown, and 50 acres of sugar beet.

Digging up beet. The crop was started as a war time measure but by 1972 this had become uneconomic and was no longer grown.

The total area farmed was over 1000 acres and by 1970 this had increased to 1287 acres.[10] Frank ran Manor Farm until 1991, when he passed the management on to his son, Martin. In 1997, Martin moved to a reconstructed farmhouse, Ivol Barn, off the road leading to Woodcote, and Christ Church sold Manor Farm house as a private residence in 1998.

Twenty years ago (2000), it was said that, Manor Farm still flourished but was fully mechanised and only employed some six persons. The village also had a dairy farm of Jersey cows with a few employees. Today (2020) the Jersey herd has long gone and the farm with modern technology requires only one worker whose time is shared with three other farms! At this point in time, (2020) South Stoke still remains an attractive rural village with its many old houses being surrounded as it is by open fields on three sides and by water meadows along the Thameside. Few who live in the village are now involved in agrarian occupations yet agriculture is luckily still all around us.

ENDNOTES:

Most of the information in this chapter is courtesy of the Victoria County History on South Stoke unless otherwise indicated.

1. Margaret Gelling in her *"Place Names of Oxfordshire"* (Cambridge University Press 1954) indicates that *"Stoc"* merely meant a place (often a religious one).

2. The Domesday Survey: The Text, in A History of the County of Oxford: Vol.1pp396-428 or online British History Online http://www.british-history.ac.uk/vch/oxon/vol1/pp396-428

Glossary
https://www.nottingham.ac.uk/manuscriptsandspecialcollections/researchguidance/manorial/glossary.aspx
Useful terms for measurement, reading documents, etc.

Also of use:- The National Archives, Glossary referring to Domesday http://www.nationalarchives.gov.uk

3. *"The Open Fields of England"* by David Hall publisher Oxford University Press 2014.
A document of 1366 in the Eynsham Cartulary refers to three fields (see Appendix 1).

4. 1818 Frederic Young map held in the archives at Christ Church, Oxford.

5. 1845 MS Estates 81 Folio 74 held in the archives at Christ Church, Oxford.

6. Reference: QS/D/A book50 Enclosure Award Book for South Stoke 28th June 1853 in The Oxfordshire Heritage Centre.

7. Bullock Family Scrapbook.

8. Comprehensive article written by Hanmer Dickson in 1989 re: The Bullock Family.

9. The Happy Circle Reminiscences of the early 1960s.

10. Bullock Family Scrapbook.

Two of the houses along The Street that had once been farms. The Malt House (above) and Fulbrook House (below)

CHAPTER 9

AN ACCOUNT OF ALE DRINKING AND BEERHOUSES WITH SOME REFERENCE TO SOUTH STOKE

C H Cook much enjoyed the village life in South Stoke and its local fishing. He was to write numerous novels and other books under the nom de plume of John Bickerdyke. *"Lady Val's Elopement"* and *"Her Wild Oats"* were two of his romantic novels set in the locality and which portray various South Stoke characters. However he also published in London in 1886 something completely different- a book entitled *"The Curiosities of Ale and Beer - An Entertaining History"*,[1] from which much of the historical information given below has been extracted. After he left the area in 1920 his house was taken over by Sir John Fox, retired Master of the Chancery Supreme Court, who was a man of wide interests, a staunch Churchman and a great supporter of village activities. The name of the house was subsequently changed from 'Willow Grange' to 'Bridleway House'.

South Stoke has always, since its earliest days, been an agricultural village, with farming and its associated trades dominating the local economy. By 1740 there was the well-established Manor Farm of some 400 acres; and in addition some 15 individual tenant farms[2], totalling some 900 acres, spread around the village and over the riverside meadows. For such a rural community the brewing and drinking of beer was a time-honoured occupation and an essential part of the diet of the hard-working farmer. Barley in those days was grown in abundance, malt was then produced at the village's *"Malt House"*, where records of tenants go back to 1706, and certainly from the 1740s maltsters are linked to this property.[3] The local water was regarded as good for brewing; hence there were no problems in regard to the brewing process. In view of all this it is of some interest to set out the general background of the ale and beer of England over the centuries, with especial reference to South Stoke.

Beer and ale have been drunk in this country since the days of the Saxon and Danish invaders, being known by the former as beer and by the latter as ale. However, the word beer seems to have been the more honourable designation, for it was said in those days that *"ale it is called among men and among the Gods beer"*. Despite that, and probably on account of the increasing influence of the Danes, the word beer gradually fell out of use and ale predominated until well after the Norman Conquest. It was a fermented drink made from malt and water, but without hops. In the 15th century the Dutch introduced a beer into England which consisted of the traditional ale, with hops added. In the 1520s story has it that a number of Flemish immigrants settled in Kent and began cultivating hops (for which that county has ever since been famous) brewing their own traditional beer. So the word beer once again became commonplace in England, in addition to the ale which was still made without hops.

Since the days of Elizabeth I (1558-1603) a system of granting licences to inns and alehouses had been introduced but this rarely reached into the countryside. It is doubtful the South Stoke establishments of the nineteenth century were in business in earlier centuries for such inns were usually found on busy coaching roads. The village of South Stoke was more of a backwater. Rather, villagers were brewing their own beer often setting up small beerhouses in their homes to meet local needs. In the reign of James I (1603-1625) a law was enacted to combat *"the loathsome and odious sin of drunkenness"*, for which a penalty of 5/- fine and six hours in the stocks was provided. Allegedly stocks were placed close to churches and in South Stoke the old stocks were situated where the lych gate now stands.

By the 17th century the word *"ale"* had become synonymous with both varieties of liquor. At that time it was described as *"our drinke which is made of barlei, water and hops, sodden and mingled together by the industrie of our bruers, in a certain exact proportion; but before our barlei do come into their hands, it sustaineth great alteration and is converted into malt"*. The use of hops was *"for the preservation of malt liquor and to communicate to it an agreable, aromatic and bitter flavour"*. Before then the fact that *"one kind of water was more suitable than another for brewing was not well understood"*. But by now *"our ancestors had learned in the school of experience that the quality of the water had much to do with the quality of the ale and beer brewed from it"; and* it was noted that *"the waters that run by chalke and cledgie* (clayey) *soils be good, and next unto the Thames water which is the most excellent"*.

In 1637, John Taylor, an old Thames waterman and innkeeper, writing in his *"Drinke and Welcome"*, had this to say of ale: *"It is called Merry-goe-downe, for it slides down merrily. It is fragrant to the scent, most pleasing to the taste ... it provokes men to singeing and mirth, which is contenting to the hearing... it doth comfort a heavy and troubled minde ... it heates the chill blood of the aged ... it is a good Whitsun Church Ale and a repairer of decayed countrey churches ... they that drinke it will reveale all they know, be it never so secret ... it will put courage into a coward ... it neither hurts nor kills any but those that abuse it"*. The same writer said that the word beer was now *"as a stranger"* and that the places where it was sold *"still retain the name of an alehouse"*. Another writer at that time described the alehouse or tavern as *"the busy man's recreation, the idle man's business, the melancholy man's sanctuary and the stranger's welcome"*.

About the year 1750 saw the introduction of porter which signified mixtures of beer which resulted in a darker and stronger brew.[4] Stout was brewed in even greater strength, with a greater proportion of hops. But, the time-honoured diet of ale and beer was being threatened, especially in the towns, by the cheap and deadly gin – *"get drunk for a penny and dead drunk for two pence"*, as the common saying went. Hogarth's prints *"Beer Street"* and *"Gin Lane"* (1751), depicted the advantages of drinking beer rather than the evil gin whilst poets often wrote on the subject of ale and beer being counteracted by the Church. If a village *"was cut off from good cheer, in the very next parish the tap may be fairish and the Vestry less bearish and stern about beer"* so wrote some nameless poet.

Up to the 17th century the brewing of ale and beer was regarded *"as the special province of the housewife and her female servants"*. It was consumed in large quantities being safer than drinking water and many villages supported two or three ale-wives, often widows, who specialised in the brewing of ale for sale.[5] Thereafter, however, all members of a family would participate in the brewing of beer, and by the 19th century it was thought most householders were doing so. In the 1840s it was said that *"there was not a labourer in his parish that did not brew his own beer"*. But by the 1880s it was reported that *"there is not one now that does it, except by chance the malt be given him"*. The reason for this was that, by the late 18th century, the commercial brewers were already becoming established. Ale was considered as a *"strong malt liquor"* being brewed in London, Burton, Derby, Manchester and Oxford whilst beer, thought a weaker *"small malt liquor"*, found favour with the brewers in Yorkshire, Nottingham and Newcastle.

In the South Oxfordshire area Brakspears of Henley dates from 1779 and Blackall Simonds of Reading from 1785 (Simonds amalgamating with Courage in 1960); whilst other breweries included Morlands of Abingdon and Morrells and Halls of Oxford. Then there were the smaller local breweries: Hilliards and Wells (taken over by Ushers in 1926) of Wallingford, and Pittmans of Goring which in 1897 became Gundrys when Ann Pittman married the brewery manager.

Gin-drinking, the scourge of the eighteenth century was seeing a resurgence in the 1820s. Spirits were cheaper than beer and the government felt that something had to be done about it. Coupled with the agricultural distress in this period they needed to alleviate the woes of the poor. Duties on malt and beer were repealed in the hope that this would combat the threat of the social ills associated with gin. More importantly The Beer-house Act of 1830 was passed allowing any person being a householder, assessed to the poor rate, to brew or sell beer by retail on payment of two guineas a year to the Excise, bypassing the jurisdiction of the magistrates. (In later years this situation was reversed.) The licence was subject to certain heavy penalties but nevertheless the licence holder could sell beer in his dwelling house whether for drinking on the premises or not. Within a few months over 24,000 beerhouse excise licences were granted. It also meant that in villages shopkeepers could open up their own beer-shop selling beer alongside their shopwares.[6] This happened in South Stoke- an 1847 directory has Mrs E. Frewin as a beer retailer (the 1841 census has William Frewin listed as a publican), Charles Wormsley was trading by 1852 and into the 1870s[7] and by 1861 Mr and later Mrs Costiff were beersellers until the 1870s.[8]

Bickerdyke states that the significance of ale and beerhouses to village life can hardly be over-emphasised. To the agricultural worker of the 19th century beer was not only a solace but an invigorating beverage, and was drunk by all in large quantities. It was an all-important item of diet almost being considered a "food", and the beerhouse was the place where *"the adult male population gathered every evening, to sip its half pints, drop by drop to make them last; and to discuss local events, wrangle over politics or farming methods"*, so wrote Flora Thompson in *"Lark Rise to Candleford"*.

The former Plough and Harrow pub in 1962

A once thatched building dating from the 17th century was The Plough and Harrow located in the centre of the village on The Street. It was held by the Clare family and was one of the houses where beer was sold for many years as a sideline to other trades. The family was listed at various times as beer retailers or licensed victuallers.[9] As early as 1840 Thomas Clare was licensed only to sell beer by retail but fell foul of the law by keeping his house open on a Sunday between the hours of 10am and 1pm. A £2 fine was his penalty.[10] When Thomas Clare the Younger died in 1858 as part of his estate there is the mention of the name The Plough and Harrow.[11] At least as early as 1864 Stephen Pemberton became the licensed victualler at the establishment.[12] He, his son Alfred and later his daughter-in-law Esther ran the pub until about 1907 but by 1911 Charles Palmer is the publican.[13]

The former Plough and Harrow in the early 20th century

Police Superintendent Porter stated in his evidence before Caversham Petty Sessions (regarding renewal of the licence) in 1911 that the "Plough and Harrow" *"had changed hands three times since 1905, but previous to then one tenant was there for nearly forty years"*[14] Charles Palmer's tenure, however, was shortlived. In May of 1911 the Licensing Authority at Oxford, (despite The Plough and Harrow having *"superior"* accommodation than The Perch and Pike and having very good sanitary arrangements) decided not to renew the license. The reason primarily *"was a want of stabling and the absence of room for vehicles to draw up"*.[15] Even then parking was a consideration!

The authorities felt with a population of 320 of which 116 were children three public houses were too much in a village the size of South Stoke. H and G Simonds had according to *"breweryhistory.com"* acquired The Plough and Harrow in 1859, their second pub in the village. It was said that competition from the two other licensed houses led to The Plough and Harrow closing for good but one brewer having two establishments in one village may well have been a factor too.

In its heyday the pub was known as *"the place where the hard drinkers always went"* [16] and incidents of drunkenness and assaults crop up in the Police Courts over the years (though to be fair The Perch and Pike was no stranger to the court system either). In 1902 when the Pembertons were still the landlords two villagers were brought before Caversham Petty Sessions for drunkenness. *"William Smith.... being drunk and disorderly...on Jan.27th. Defendant did not appear. P.C. Eden said the defendant was ejected from "The Plough and Harrow". He wanted to fight. Fined 5s. or five days. Mrs Alice Maskell,...was summoned for a similar offence on the same occasion. She pleaded not guilty. P.C.*

Lambourn said the defendant snatched hold of his cape and tore it and also used bad language. She was drunk. A fine of 5s.was imposed".[17] Today it has long since been a private house but remains an attractive, painted brick and timbered building with old tile roof, listed Grade II and known as Plough Cottage.

The former Plough and Harrow today with the Perch and Pike pub beyond

The Perch and Pike was not only one of the competitors of The Plough and Harrow, but was also located next door to that pub and was possibly contemporary in age. The solid flint and brick building, with old tile roof, however, is not as picturesque since the 1969 two storey brick extension was added.[18] It could have served as a beerhouse but the earliest found records date from around the 1881 census showing Frederick Staden as *"beerseller"*. The word *"publican"* being crossed out. Mr Staden was even listed earlier in the Trade Directories from 1877 until 1883 as a beer retailer.[19] 1886 has the name *"Bricklayers Arms"* for this establishment and two years later the Goring Brewery (Pittman's) was seeking to let the business along with 5 acres of *"Garden and Arable land"*.[20] (One of the fields to the north of the village was known as Brick Kiln Field or Brick Field Acre where bricks used to be ploughed up. Whether local bricks were made here is now not known).[21] Kelly's Directory of 1887 mentions Thomas Gardner as a beer retailer but it seems his time was shortlived. Francis Leigh Vickery became the new *"beerhouse keeper"* and by 1891 the *"Bricklayers Arms"* had become the Perch and Pike.[22] However for renewing licences the name Bricklayers Arms was still being referred to as late as 1911.[23]

Early image of the Perch and Pike

In 1887, Mrs Pittman was advertising to sell her brewery and her estate of 37 licensed houses which included four pubs in Goring, Ye Olde Leatherne Bottel and The Perch and Pike. However, it was called off some months later for Mrs Pittman decided to continue to run the business with the help of her daughter Ann. In 1897 Ann married the brewery's manager, Mr Gundry, and between them they continued to run what was now Gundry's Brewery until Ann died many years later. In 1940 Gundry's Brewery and all the public houses including The Perch and Pike was sold to Brakspears Brewery. In 2002, W.H. Brakspear & Sons licensed the brewing of its beers to Refresh UK, owner of Wychwood Brewery, and the brewery ceased production and closed. Though no longer a major brewer in Henley, apart from small premises in Bell Street, Brakspears still retain their pubs. (2020)

As the Goring and Streatley History Society's *'Picture History'* has recorded, *"Gundry's beer had a fine reputation: the water came from the brewery's own well in the High Street, a donkey being used to bring up the buckets, and special barley was grown at Park Farm for the malt"*. As the South Stoke History Society's *"Trades and Traders"* has described, *"the Perch and Pike was fondly remembered by older villagers as the first port of call in the early years of the (twentieth) century, with beer being served from 7 a.m. to 10 p.m. and costing only 2d a pint. An increase to 3d during World War I was considered a grave blow"*. In the early years of the twentieth century it was thought that there were some *"15 local farms and beerhouses in the village, all of which brewed and sold their own beer to refresh thirsty labourers"*. This cannot be verified.

Francis L. Vickery remained the landlord until at least 1907 [24] but by 1911 Albert Poffley was the *"licensed victualler"*. 1917 saw William Rose in charge until at least 1924.[25] Albert Wickens appears to be the landlord possibly in the 1920s to at least 1935.[26] A Directory of

1939 has Edwin W. Rouse (Bill) running The Perch and Pike and certainly his wife was still there as late as 1965.[27]

Mr and Mrs Bill Rouse arm in arm outside the entrance to the Perch and Pike

A W.I. member, writing about South Stoke after the last war, had this to say about it: *"An old inn called the Perch and Pike stands further up The Street, a homely place for visitors and an inn where old friends meet"*. An Oxford Times reporter, who *"dropped in on South Stoke"* in July 1961, to write a story about the village, did of course visit the pub; where he found *"a fascinating old musical box, the size of a small radiogram, which customers can play by putting 1d in the slot"*. As he entered, the machine *"was tinkling its way through an enchanting melody"*, that was *"vastly preferable to the modern juke box"*. The pub had a fine stuffed pike in a glass case, and the reporter was soon *"regaled with fishing stories"*. With updating and decorating the pub and the comings and goings of numerous landlords the glass case has disappeared (2020). In those days pubs were essentially male-dominated and frequented by the ardent beer drinker.

Cyril Ireson became the landlord from 1968 and ran the pub for over 5 years until Reg and Sylvia Harper took over in 1973. When they left in 1986 it was still a pub with the emphasis on drink and limited availability of food. The Mason-Apps took over with new ideas and a younger outlook. Regrettably, the pub was closed down in August of 1992[27a]. When the pub reopened in January 1993 it was with new tenants, Mike and Jill Robinson. Food was definitely on the menu by now and they ran a professional business. At this point the old barn was still just that. It would not be until after they left in 1999 that the brewery took up their idea of rebuilding the barn and creating a restaurant and kitchen area with bedrooms to let above. With high rents from the brewery the following decade saw seven struggling landlords come and go. 2013 saw new tenants, Alex and Kim Koniotes, and a new refurbishment jointly paid for by the tenants and Brakspears. They stayed less than three years, for a publican's life is hard. 2016 brought Simon Duffy and his partner and young family to the Perch and Pike but a new tenant is already ensconced. (2020). It appears that gone are the days when a publican stayed long term.[28]

The third and it seems the earliest public house in the nineteenth century was the Cross Keys (being the symbol of St Peter who, together with his brother St Andrew, is depicted in the stained glass East window of St Andrew's Church). The Cross Keys was also the arms of the Papal See. (*"Inns, Ales and Drinking Customs of Old England"* by Frederick W. Hackwood p 301). A former owner of The Cross Keys when it was a house (though still with the pub layout) was John Martin.

View of the former Cross Keys pub from the railway embankment, c.1970s

He wrote the following information some twenty years ago. The detail is so specific and he cites as his sources *"Deeds etc. of the Cross Keys, Victuallers Recognizances, Parish Records' Abstract, and GPO Directories, GWR Map of land purchase, sale catalogues of Brewery, Various Village Scrapbooks and reminiscences"*. Unfortunately finding this information for verification purposes is proving illusory particularly with regard to the 18th century evidence however it should be recorded as a possible history:-

A Cross Keys *"was built in 1813 on a site previously occupied by two cottages dating from around 1738, at the intersection of a road, which once ran along the line of the present railway and served the fields to the north and south of the village, with the Cross Keys Road. It seems that one of those cottages had, since 1787, been in use as a beerhouse, being known as the Windmill (on account of the fact that, on a hill due south east of that beerhouse and easily seen from its site, there was in mediaeval times a windmill used by the villagers of South Stoke for grinding their corn). As recorded in the booklet "Trades and Traders" the Cross Keys was leased to Blackall Simonds, the Reading Brewers."*

The book of Victuallers' Recognizances for 1801-1822 states John Allom runs The Windmill in South Stoke and that between 1812-1817 there appear to be gaps in the record. Could this have been when a new building was erected? Certainly when the records appear again in 1818 The Windmill is now The Cross Keys and Blackall Simonds is one offering a surety for Mr Allom.[29]

"It is said that for a time the pub was rented to the G.W.R. to accommodate workmen" at a time when the railway was being built through the village in the late 1830s but there is no documentation found for this.

A brewery map of 1866 shows The Cross Keys building aligned east-west whereas an 1877 map has the alignment in a north-south direction. An old villager recorded that the pub was originally at the side of the road and that it had burned down. In 1870 Simonds Brewery took the GWR to court over a spark from a railway engine allegedly setting fire to the thatched part of the roof on the pub the previous year. *"The premises were destroyed"*. However, one witness claimed that the pub was in a *"tumbledown state and the gable end fell down a year before"*. The brewery won their case but only received

£200 in damages, far less than they were seeking.[30] The pub appears to continue functioning so it is assumed the brewery rebuilt or patched up the pub.

In 1892 there were further changes when land was bought from the Brewery by the G.W.R. in order to widen the railway line from two tracks to four tracks, taking up much of what had been the forecourt of the pub and bringing the railway line even closer to the building.

The licensees recorded over the years were:-

From at least 1801- John Allom who was the landlord when it was known as The Windmill. He was still there in 1821 and by then the pub was known as The Cross Keys.

c.1847-1852 Joseph Panter,[31]

c.1853-1863 Sophia Neal,[32]

1864 John Chandler,[33]

1867-c.1895 Henry Green,[34]

1897-c.1901 Benjamin Allum,[35]

c.1903-c.1920 Walter Smith,[36] followed by his son, Arthur Edward Smith for a time,

Then by at least 1928-1935 Henry Thomas Couling,[37]

c.1939-1954 Arthur Edward Smith,[38]

And c.1955-58 J.D. Turner.

The 1960s were increasingly difficult for John T Gage and finally Ernest C. G. Bird.[39]

The Cross Keys closed its doors on 10th January 1967 when it was sold off as a private house,

The earlier reference to *"thirsty labourers being refreshed by beer"* is of interest and in this connection it is relevant to quote from Adrian Bell's *"The Open Air – An Anthology of English Country Life"* (Faber and Faber 1936). There he describes how, between the wars, a hayfield would be cut by a line of men with scythes, starting at sunrise. At around midday, *"elevenses -Blessed word"*, a cart would arrive with the wives, farm ladies and boys, *"bringing the half of a 40lb cheese, a large batch of bread and an 18 gallon cask of home-brewed beer"*. Jars of beer would then be passed around. Thereafter, *"as the jars empty and the bread and cheese disappears, the women go to the cart for fresh supplies, whilst the men slice the onions brought out in baskets from their own gardens; whilst a screw of baccy tops the meal. With this in their pipes they rest thankfully until it is time to go back to work"*. Small wonder that a Ploughman's is still a popular item of bar food to this day!

Beer also has a traditional association with the Church. Regular meetings of the Vestry (the forerunner of the Parish Council and the Parochial Church Council.) were often held in the local beerhouses, where *"ale was often drunk"* to enliven the discussions. As one attending such meetings has recorded; *"ale is the liquor makes our tongues run quick"*. Earlier, in mediaeval times, the Church often had to resort to a variety of money-raising schemes. *"One of the most interesting was that of holding a Church Ale; the Warden begging or buying the malt and then brewing the liquor in the church House (the prototype of today's Parish Hall), which was then sold on special occasions"*. There is no reason to suppose that South Stoke did not also resort to such Church Ales. However in 1603 Church Ales were forbidden and in many cases failed to survive Cromwell's Interregnum with the Church becoming more opposed to the use of drink.

John Bickerdyke had this to say about Church Ales, of which the Easter and Whitsun Ales were the most important. The money raised was *"to repair the Churches and Chapels buy bookes for service, cuppes for celebration of the Sacrament, surpluses for Sir John and other necessaries"*. The Church Ale was usually celebrated in the Church House, which was either hired for the occasion or was one over which the Church had some right. The Bishop of Bath and Wells, writing in the 16th century, referred to the event as *"when the people went from afternoon prayers on Sundays to their lawful sports and pastimes in the churchyard or in the neighbourhood, where they drank and made merry. By the benevolence of the people many poor parishes have cast their bells, beautified their churches and raised stock for the poor"*. Then there was the annual Tithe Ale, a repast of bread, cheese and ale, provided by the recipient of the tithe and much enjoyed by the tithe payers. There was also the old saying, *"Old England's cheer is beef and beer"*; and it should be remembered that, before tea and coffee were available, *"ale was the morning drink for both squire and yeoman"*.

John Bickerdyke refers to the occasions of feasting for all: *"New Year's Eve and Day, a time for wassailing and carol singing";* Twelfth Night, especially celebrated with wassailing and the consumption of spiced cakes, giving rise to the phrase "*cakes and ale*"; Plough Monday, when a dressed up plough was taken from house to house and when bread, cheese and ale were provided; Easter Monday and Tuesday, which were noted for the custom of "*heaving*"; May Day, which was the most joyous and picturesque of all; Whitsuntide, a time for Whitsun Ales, Church Ales and Morris Dancers; Haymaking, when the harvest was gathered in the merry month of June; and finally Christmas, a time of carol singing and good cheer'.

Also Harvest Home celebrations:-

'Come all my Lads and Lasses, Let us together go,

To the pleasant cornfield, Our courage for to show,

With sickle and with knapsack, So well we clear our land,

The Farmer crys "Work on Boys, here's Beer at your command",

In a good old Leather Bottle, of ale that is so brown,

We'll cut and strip together, Until the sun goes down.

It is worth recalling that a Memory of South Stoke's Happy Circle Club tells us that a Wake, called the Revels, was held in the village every year on the Monday fortnight after Whitsun; and was attended by people from neighbouring villages and by visitors. Stalls were set up in The Street, whilst in the yard of the Perch and Pike there were swingboats, and coconut shies in the field by the Vicarage. Much beer was drunk and these revels became very lively affairs, so that often parents would not allow their children to attend. They were held for the last time around 1910. At such festivities popular songs concerning ale and beer were often sung.

Two nearby pubs that were once popular with the locals are the Leatherne Bottle, beside the Thames on the bridlepath between South Stoke and Goring, and the Beetle and Wedge on the river, at Moulsford. However, both, over the years, have been developed into smart riverside restaurants, with the emphasis on good food.

The traditional atmosphere and character of an English pub has been well described by the writer, Ernest Baker, in his book *"The Character of England"*, published in 1950 by Readers' Union. The public house, he wrote, *"is second only to hearth and home as the most popular English indoor recreation ... The opening hours, so peculiar to English life, have at least the effect of ensuring a concerted attendance , and so a social event ... The social event is the thing; darts, skittles and billiards are all secondaries. It is the play of the personalities and the opportunity of hospitality to others which draws men to their circle. The colour lies in tone of voice and dialect, and in the counterpoint of interruption; the brilliance lies in the gusto of fresh anecdote and meeting. .... English beer may be no longer what it was, but even so, it is not difficult to understand why the pub remains the most popular of all English recreations*".

The Perch and Pike in 2020 is South Stoke's only pub. Times have changed and today the Perch and Pike offers not only the traditional Brakspear's ales, but also a wide range of spirits, together with a variety of the now popular lager beers. It is increasingly popular with weekend visitors, who drive in from nearby towns and villages; and also with hikers using the Ridgeway Path, which runs right past the pub. Such visitors are attracted not only by the character of the pub and its drinks, but also by its selection of foods, available in a restaurant that is on the site of the old barn. After so many years of being excluded from the male-dominated pub clientele, women of all ages are now equally welcome, whether they be on their own or accompanied. In the summer months the bar overflows on to chairs and benches outside, in the forecourt and in the garden; whilst in the winter time the bar, well heated by an attractive log fire, can usually accommodate all its customers.

The Perch and Pike showing the replaced modern barn extension linked to the pub. Today this is a restaurant with letting rooms above.

ENDNOTES:

1. *"Curiosities of Ale and Beer: An Entertaining History"* by John Bickerdyke first published in 1889 but reprinted into the 21st century. (BeerBooks.com 2008).

2. Victoria County History under South Stoke.

3. The Malt House Indenture housed at The Malt House South Stoke (2020).

4. *"Inns, Ales and Drinking Customs of Old England"* by Frederick W Hackwood p.100.

5. *"The English Village"* by Richard Muir p.92.

6. Brewery History Society Journal (2015) article by Eric Tenbus re: The Beerhouse Act of 1830 and historyhouse.co.uk re: Beerhouses and Beershops.

7. 1852 Directory, 1854 P.O.Directory of Berks. Northants., 1864,1869 Directory and the 1871 Census.

8. 1861 and 1871 Census and Jackson's Oxford Journal 25th March 1871.

9. 1847 PO. Directory, Gardner's Directory of 1852.

10. Oxfordshire Heritage Centre QS1840/3/L1/20 Conviction of Thomas Clare in 1840.

11. England and Wales National Probate Calendar 1858-1966, 1973-1995.

12. Directory for 1864, 1871 Census.

13. Kelly's Directory 1907.

14. 1911 Census, Henley and South Oxford Standard 17th March 1911.

15. Oxfordshire Weekly News 17th May 1911.

16. Oral interview with Jean Dixon nee Allum.

17. Reading Mercury 15th February 1902.

18. SODC planning application for The Perch and Pike P69/H0056.

19. P.O. Directory of Oxfordshire 1877, Kelly's Directory of Berks., Bucks. & Oxon. 1883.

20. Reading Mercury et al.8th September 1888.

21. Oral recollection of George Druce. The Victoria County History refers to brickworks at Greenmoor Hill which had been there since at least 1742. MS.Top.Oxon.c.357,f.68.

22. 1891 Census.

23. Henley and South Oxford Standard 17th March 1911.

24 1907 Trades Directory.

25. 2nd February 1917 Berkshire and Oxfordshire Advertiser.

26. Oxfordshire Heritage Centre PAR254\17\2\E1\1-2 List of houses and occupants in 1935.

27. 25th September 1965 Reading Mercury.

27a. Brakspear's records of the chronology of the Perch and Pike Licensees, states "VAT Man Closure..."

28. Information provided by Brakspears Brewery.

29. Q5D/V4 Victuallers' Recognizances 1801-1822 Oxfordshire Heritage Centre.

30. Oxford Chronicle/Reading Gazette 16th July 1870.

31. P.O. Directory of 1847, Gardner-History, Gazetteer & Directory of the County of Oxford 1852.

32. Sophia Neal -Lascelle's Oxon. Directory 1853, The PO Directory of Berks. and Northants.1854, the Census of 1861 classed as innkeeper in South Stoke, Dutton Allen & Co. Directory of Oxon. & Berks.1863.

33. John Chandler – 1864 Directory.

34. Henry Green – Directories of 1869, 1876 and Kelly's Directory of 1895. Censuses of 1871-1891.

35. Benjamin Allum- The Berkshire Chronicle 19th March 1898 states he is The Cross Keys landlord (Railway Fatality), Census of 1901.

36. Walter Smith – Kelly's Directories of 1903.1907, 1911 and 1915.

37. Henry Thomas Couling - Kelly's Directories 1928-to at least 1935.

38. Arthur Edward Smith - Census of 1911. Moved out of the pub living in the village but had returned by 1939 staying until 1954 - Oral interview of Dorothy Smith (step daughter).

39. British Phone Books 1880-1984 1957,1958,1963,1964.

As an aside, Ridgeway Brewing Ltd. is South Stoke's current commercial brewing operation. The office is in Chapel Close but the brewing is undertaken out of county. It was set up by Brakspear's former head brewer, Peter Scholey, specialising in bottled conditioned beers although cask beers are occasionally available at beer festivals and locally. CAMRA Good Beer Guide 2020.

CHAPTER 10

SOUTH STOKE AND THE RAILWAY

Whilst the River Thames slips past the western boundary of the parish without fuss and largely unheeded, the railway line, on its embankment, is a major feature, within sight of a large proportion of the dwellings and certainly within earshot of the vast majority. Built in the late 1830s its slightly curving route appears to cradle the village as it existed at that time as if in the crook of its arm. Not everyone views it so poetically as the majority of later development of the village, much of it originally what is now termed social housing, took place to the east of the railway and this has occasionally led to a polarisation of attitudes between *"them"* and *"us"* depending on which side of the tracks one lives.

The concept

In the early 1800s, Bristol was a major port which was already linked to London by the Kennet & Avon Canal and the Thames but railways were being developed and were demonstrating their superiority in terms of speed and availability, waterways being at the mercy of frost, drought and flood. By 1832 there were already plans for railways to link Liverpool to Birmingham and Birmingham to London which would potentially enable Liverpool to eclipse Bristol as the major Atlantic port in England. A small group of Bristol businessmen, alarmed at this, garnered support amongst fellow merchants to underwrite a preliminary route survey and cost estimate for a railway to link the cities of Bristol and London, and appointed Isambard Kingdom Brunel as engineer on 7th March 1832.

Planning the route

Two routes were examined in detail, one to the south through Devizes, the Vale of Pewsey, and Newbury, roughly following the same route as the Kennet & Avon Canal; the other through Chippenham, Swindon and the Vale of the White Horse. As this latter route had easier gradients, as well as providing the possibility of future links to Oxford, plus Gloucester and hence into South Wales, it was recommended by Brunel and accepted by the sponsors who then presented it at a public meeting on 30th July 1833. That meeting resolved to create a committee to take the project forward by seeking funding and obtaining the necessary Act of Parliament. First mentioned as such in Brunel's Journals on 27th August 1833, the *"London & Bristol Railway"* was henceforward to be known as the *"Great Western Railway"*, (GWR).

Presenting the Act required detailed surveys of the entire route and Brunel's journals record a hectic period of surveying activity, but one entry in particular might be seen to have set the seal on the future railway route impinging on South Stoke rather than remaining on the west bank of the Thames as originally intended. On 15th September 1833 he wrote *"Rode on to Streatley; tried in every way to find a line round instead of crossing the river at Goring; found it impossible"*.

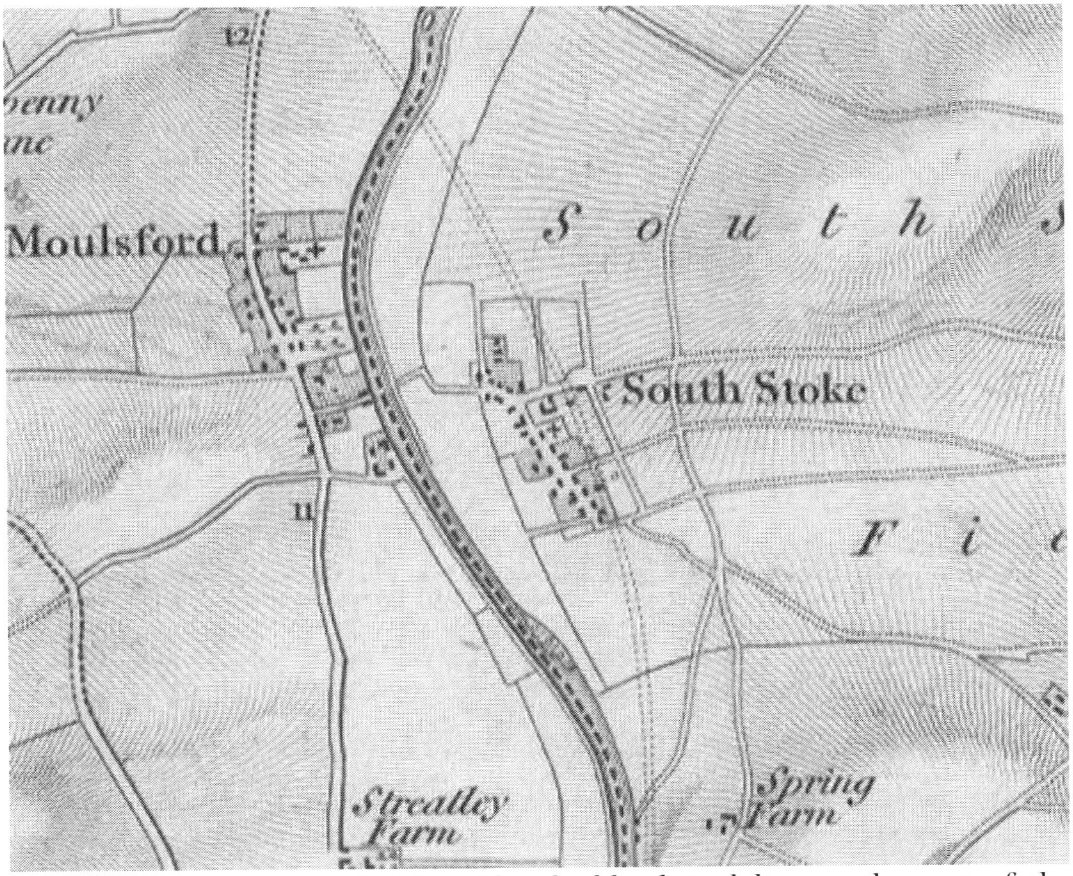

Ordnance survey map of 1833. The double dotted line to the east of the village became the route of the railway crossing the Thames to the north.

Opposition

It may seem strange but there was significant opposition to the building of the railway from some of the local towns which might have benefitted – Abingdon and Wallingford were included on original concept lines - but through outright opposition, mainly from landowners, or just apathy, they were scrubbed from the plans and a more sweeping line to the west was followed. It was, however, always in Brunel's mind to connect these places by branches at a future date. This did eventually happen, though they never reaped the benefits that a direct link on the main line itself might have provided.

Others, who saw the proposed railway as a threat to their own businesses, were equally hostile – none more so than the Thames Commissioners who foresaw a massive reduction in their income from existing barge traffic, particularly from Bristol and the west via the Kennet & Avon canal, whose proprietors were obviously similarly alarmed by the proposals.

A high speed railway

From the outset Brunel intended that the Great Western Railway would be engineered to achieve as high a speed as possible. To this end the route chosen avoided, as far as it could, any excessive gradients. Indeed over the section from London Paddington to Didcot the gradient is never more than 1 in 1320 (0.075%), and from there to Swindon less than 1 in 660 (0.15%) and was considered, for train planning purposes, as *"level"*, earning the line the accolade of *"Brunel's Billiard Table"*. However, this level could not be maintained west of Swindon where, because of the terrain, there are more severe gradients, even up to 1 in 100 (1%) for short sections. Furthermore the curves of the line are as gentle as possible to facilitate fast running.

Part of the plan to enable higher speeds and greater comfort was to build the railway to a broader track gauge – the distance between the two rails - of 7ft (2,134 mm) as opposed to the 4ft 8½ins

(1,435 mm) which had already become the norm elsewhere. There had been some sleight of hand in not defining the gauge in the Act of Parliament (31st August 1835) where it might have elicited more opposition.

Intended to make the ride more comfortable by making the road-bed more stable the track itself was laid, not on stone blocks as was the fashion of the time, nor the transverse sleepers with which we are familiar today, but on longitudinal timber baulks with the inter-rail spacing maintained by cross-ties between them. This was fortuitous as Brunel, who did make occasional mistakes, found that he had not allowed for a non-binding fit between wheel and rail on curves when he had ordered the initial locomotives so, when they were delivered, he took the pragmatic expedient of packing the cross-ties to ease the gauge to 7ft 0¼in (2,140 mm) and subsequently built the rest of the GWR to that gauge!

Examples of bridge rails

To complete the trackwork Brunel also designed a new type of rail called *"Bridge Rail"*, which was developed in various weights as experience and economy dictated. Much was later re-used as fence posts and notice poles around the railway and many examples can still be found in the village (page 131 shows rails as fence posts).

Building the line

Work on the railway was started from both ends (Bristol and London) and the initial section from London to Taplow was opened in June 1838, to Twyford in December 1839, and to Reading in March 1840. Meanwhile the route westwards beyond Reading had been finalised and surveyed in detail, contracts had been advertised and let, and work was in progress by this latter date.

The Contract (2R) for Moulsford Bridge (known here in the village as the *"Four Arches"*) had been advertised locally in March 1837 and was subsequently allocated, together with that for the Gatehampton river bridge (1R), to William Chadwick, who was already building the Maidenhead river bridge, famous for its flat arch.

Contract 3R for the *"excavation and formation of all the earthworks and the construction of all Bridges, Culverts and Brickwork and Masonry and the entire completion (excepting the laying of permanent rails) of that portion of the line from the Bridge ..... now building over the River Thames at Gatehampton .... to the Bridge over the River Thames at Moulsford ..... about 3 miles and 24 chains"*, i.e. the cuttings and embankments

View of the embankment at the southern end of the village. The two properties to the left are former farm workers' cottages

One of the three original Brunel railway bridges allowing access to the village

between the two river crossings, so including *"our"* bit within the parish, was advertised in February 1838 and let to Richard Custance of Goring for a final price of £26,455.0s.6d.

The section within the parish is all on an embankment, formed of material dug from the cutting excavated for the line to the south of the village towards Goring. The cuttings and the embankment here, and at Gatehampton, largely equated in volume, with provision to bring any additional material required for the embankments from the cuttings between Basildon and Pangbourne. The embankment crosses the three roads into the village (South Bank, Cross Keys Road and Ferry Road) so that three bridges under the rail line had to be constructed. There is also one culvert for a spring-fed stream at the very southern boundary of the Parish, near the Withymead nature reserve, and what might be better described as a pedestrian tunnel rather than a bridge - locally called the *"Bogey hole"* - where a footpath linking South Stoke to Little Stoke is crossed. All of these bridges are of a standard form and built simply at right angles to the railway line.

As stated, Contract 3R was essentially for the ground works and excluded the laying of the rails. This work was contracted separately and the whole line from London to Didcot was the subject of two contracts let to John Shedlock. The line was laid on ballast, including gravel extracted from land obtained for the purpose locally, though some was also dredged from the river hereabouts. The specification of the rails and the longitudinal timbers had evolved from that originally used, and the rail was now specified as 62 pounds per yard rail laid on 14 inch wide by 7 inch deep baulks with the appropriate cross-ties.

Moulsford Bridge – The Four Arches

The original Brunel-designed Moulsford Bridge

As it is readily accessible from the old towing path, which now forms a footpath route from the village towards North Stoke and Crowmarsh, the beauty of this bridge is easily appreciated, both in its overall setting and on closer scrutiny. Of particularly striking visual interest is the graceful diagonal arching brickwork. The original bridge, on the downstream side, is paralleled by a second companion to the same design upstream, built when the lines were quadrupled in the 1890s, albeit with slightly less embellishments, lacking the Bath stone facings of the original.

Whilst, particularly when viewed from underneath, the bridge appears massive and solid the actual structure, particularly above the arches, is a honeycomb of galleries, which give it strength without excessive weight.

The building of a bridge necessitated the construction of significant timber formers, known as *"centrings"*, which supported the shape of the arches until they were completed and the stone and brickwork became interlocked and self-supporting. The construction of these centrings, together with associated staging, plus work surrounding the building of the piers, inevitably constrained the available channels for boats and, this, together with issues related to the obstruction of the towing paths at both river crossings, brought Brunel into regular conflict with the Thames Commissioners. He evidently held them in little regard, treating them to the very shortest of responses to their complaints.

Navvies – the men who built the railway (by hand)

The canal building age from the mid-1700s created a demand for human brawn to accomplish these great works using pick, shovel and wheelbarrow. These mainly itinerant workers – termed navigators (navvies) as they were building new navigations - moving from contract to contract, gained a reputation for hard work, accompanied by hard drinking and rowdy behaviour. The end of canal building was followed by the railway age and human muscle was therefore still much in demand to carry out these works, with large armies of labourers employed on the contracts here, both experienced men and ex-agricultural labourers recruited locally.

Whilst we have found no specific records of the experience (good or bad) of the interface between this village and the navvies we do have insights from recorded events in both Moulsford and Goring. The Rev. Lloyd of Moulsford wrote, *"They appeared to be living without God in the world and yet I ought to bear my testimony to their general civility and good behaviour to my own parishioners, and also to myself"*. As he also references his experience of having the men billeted there for 2 years it may be that they included more skilled and, perhaps, more sober, men (carpenters, bricklayers and stone masons) working on the river bridge rather than just navvies.

There was some trouble in the autumn of 1839 in Goring but a report to the Directors from the resident engineer suggests that other local tensions may have led to some of the issues being wrongly attributed to the navvies. He states, *"...a very serious feud exists between (the Vicar) and his parishioners...... There was much rioting in the Parish in consequence.... I mention this because I think (the Vicar) over estimates the amount of rioting and places it, as is usual, to the score of the Navigators"*.

Whilst we have no direct local evidence, it is likely that, as counterpoint to the disturbance caused by such behaviour, some local people would have been able to profit from the influx of the workers, none more so than those running any business selling ale! In addition, the railway company was opposed to the *"truck"* system where unscrupulous employers, instead of using cash, would pay their workforce in goods or in tokens which could only be used in the shops owned by the employers. So far as it was able the Great Western Company prevented the use of this practice by its contractors. Thus the navvies were free to choose where they spent their pay and were not just confined to purchasing from a company-controlled supplier.

However, all good things come to an end and as the contracts were completed the navvies moved on, sometimes to other contracts with the same employer, sometimes to new works starting in other parts of the country. Some of these opportunities were advertised in newspapers in this area as contracts here were known to be coming to completion, such as *"Northern & Eastern Railway. To Navigators. Wanted 800 good able bodied men. Apply Mr McKeane at Roydon Burnt Mill, Harlow or Sawbridgeworth"*. (This was, incidentally, another slightly unusual, railway, being built to a gauge of 5 feet (1524mm).)

Opening of the line – 1st June 1840

On Sunday 31st May 1840 the directors of the company, together with their guests, travelled on a special train hauled by a brand new locomotive, the first of the Firefly Class, *Charon,* completing the journey from London to Steventon (the new, but temporary) terminus in an hour and ten minutes. After a lunch they returned to London and thus set the seal on the official opening to the public the next day when the advertised timetable service began. The stations at Steventon and Moulsford were built adjacent to turnpikes to afford road coach connections respectively to Abingdon and Oxford, and Wallingford and Oxford. They were besieged by the public, some wanting to travel but most just wanting to gaze on the new wonder.

Following official representations from Wallingford the station initially called Moulsford was renamed *"Wallingford Road"* on 6th October 1840 to perhaps better describe its commercial purpose, serving the town of Wallingford rather than a small rural village which would have struggled to generate any traffic itself.

The situation at Goring station, which had been provided with minimal facilities, was so dire as far as originating traffic was concerned that there was serious consideration given by the directors of the company to closing it. Part of the reason may have been that there were such limited facilities at Goring – just a *"Booking Shed"* and a platform.

While it may seem unusual to us, at other larger stations, facilities were provided for the conveyance of the personal carriages (that is horse-drawn carriages) of the passengers and, if they so wished, their own horses. The inevitable delays that occurred in loading and unloading these caused the company to limit the number of trains serving some of the intermediate stations, like Wallingford Road, so as not to completely upset the overall timetable.

The initial timetable was for 8 passenger and 2 goods trains per day each way with the earliest Up (towards London) train starting from Steventon at 3.15am and carrying the Mail, with the latest (a goods train) leaving at 9.40pm. In the Down direction the first was a goods train leaving London at 4.00am and the last, a passenger train (also conveying Mail), at 9.05pm.

Health and safety

The perception of the 1830s and 1840s, when the initial build phase was in full swing, is that there was little concern for the safety and well-being of workers. Indeed there is plenty of evidence of accidents and fatalities. However, the Great Western Railway insisted that all incidents had to be reported to and recorded by the resident engineer. The records were then forwarded to Brunel who examined the circumstances and made recommendations to avoid repeat occurrences.

That said, the company had a policy of insisting that casualties were only to be taken to medical facilities to which they had subscribed. This often led to the injured having to be conveyed long distances in carts over poor roads, with inevitable results. Those injured locally were taken to the Reading Dispensary in Chain Street or, after it opened in May 1839, to the then new Royal Berkshire Hospital.

It was the custom that the workers themselves subscribed to a form of *"Sick Club"* which ensured that any of their number who was temporarily unable to work could still get some small payment to cover bare essentials. In the event of a fatal accident, if they were aware of the existence of family, they might provide a donation to the bereaved relatives.

Further research is required but, to date, we know of only one fatal accident from the initial build phase where the unfortunate victim is buried here in the village. He was 17-year-old William Hardaker who was killed when *"a railroad waggon ran over him"*. This would have been one of the horse-drawn spoil wagons running on temporary rails from the cuttings to the tip-head where the embankment was being formed.

The completion of this phase was not the end of accidents, as further serious injuries and fatalities would occur on and about the railway in operation, initially because people were oblivious to the dangers. One of the first was on 19th August 1840, when 54 year-old Joseph Pearce was run over and killed by the engine *"Tiger"*. He was from London and had been visiting relatives here in the village but had decided to use the railway as a walking route.

There were also consequences in South Stoke for the railway passing through the village's farmland and the occasional property. In 1868 a field of barley was allegedly burnt due to a spark thrown out by a passing engine. Then in September of the following year the thatched roof of The Cross Keys pub was thought to have caught alight by a spark from a train going up to London. Thirty years earlier the brewery as a precaution against sparks had removed part of the thatched roof and replaced it with slate tiles. However, this time Simonds Brewery took GWR to court seeking damages against the pub's destruction. Naturally GWR denied that it had been a spark and although the brewery was awarded some damages it was nothing like the amount they were seeking and it does not appear to have been a conclusive decision. (Oxford Chronicle and Reading Gazette 16th July 1870).

The later Moulsford Bridge built to provide additional lines in the 1890s

There were more accidents when the new bridge was being built to accommodate the new pair of lines. In 1891 Tom Hann fell off the bridge into the river and was drowned, his body not being found for 4 weeks. No relatives were known and he is also buried here in St Andrew's churchyard.

On Saturday 9th May 1899 39 year-old labourer James Pearce, who lived in the village, was killed by being run down by an express from

Penzance near Goring station. Having been seen to set off walking along the road, no-one was able to explain why he came to be on the railway, except that he may have decided to take a short cut. The verdict of the inquest was *"Accidental death through imprudence in trespassing on the railway"*.

Also interred in the churchyard, and recorded on the War Memorial, as he was on active service, is Private Benjamin Norman Palmer, ASC (Army Service Corps), who somehow fell from a train on 19th September 1914 whilst on his way from Aldershot to Warwick to take up a posting. At the inquest it was supposed that he may have been intending to go to use the toilet but, in the dark, opened the external door instead, fell out, and was then run over by a freight train on the adjacent line. His grave is marked by a standard War Graves Commission headstone.

The railway in use

Whilst the section of line here had now come into daily use, work continued on further sections both from this end heading west and from the Bristol end heading east. Just 7 weeks after the opening to Steventon the line was opened further to Farringdon Road and, by the end of the year, to Hay Lane (Wootton Bassett Road). The completion of work enabled the whole route between Bristol and London to be opened on 20th June 1841. From that date the local population became spectators as the Great Western Railway evolved, with increasing traffic, at increasing speeds, and using developing technology.

Local newspapers seem to confirm that train spotting had already begun, with various letters to the Editor mentioning specific engines. The GWR did not number their broad gauge locos but only gave them names, some inspiring, some unusual, and some quite obscure.

The gauge issue

As the GWR and associated companies developed their broad gauge network beyond the initial Bristol to London main line they faced the issue of interface with other railways built to the narrower gauge. This inevitably meant passengers changing from one train to another and goods having to be transhipped between wagons on the two systems. This became a serious issue and a Royal Commission on Railway Gauges was set up to examine the situation and recommend the way forward. As part of the process, comparative trials, suggested by Brunel, were conducted between the two systems and the GWR Broad Gauge tests took place in 1845 with *Ixion*, a Firefly Class locomotive, which achieved speeds of over 60 mph with various loads. These trials took place between Paddington and Didcot so would have been witnessed by South Stoke residents. The narrow gauge comparative trials, run over lines with similar characteristics, were dogged by problems with the locomotives, one even falling off the track. In essence the outcome of these runs was that the broad gauge was plainly superior. However, the Commission ruled in favour of what would become the "standard" gauge, mainly because of the much greater mileage of that system already in operation and the significantly greater cost that would arise in converting these lines if the 7-foot system were adopted, especially the need to take extra land to extend the width of the track-bed.

The outcome in the short term was that certain lines, to be used by trains built to both gauges, had a third rail added so that one rail (that nearest any station platform) was used by both and then there were two other rails – the original broad gauge one, and another to allow the "standard gauge" vehicles to use the line. Eventually it was accepted that it would indeed become the standard, even on the GWR, and the final broad gauge train left Paddington to pass the village on Friday 20th May 1892.

Section of a dual gauge railway with a third rail

You may hear people say that *"they converted the whole GWR system in one weekend"*. This is patently untrue as there was no conversion work to be done on much of the track mileage since it was already by then mostly dual gauge and certainly there would not have been hordes of track workers on the line here over that May weekend. Significant work had to be done in the far south west where dual gauge track had not been installed and gangs of skilled men from elsewhere on the system were shipped in to make the changes in a very well organised and executed process over that weekend.

Interestingly, the Wallingford branch line, which had opened in July 1866, was built to the standard gauge, partly for reasons of economy in land acquisition by the local funders, but also because the GWR main line here had recently been converted to mixed gauge. The branch ran from the Wallingford Road station alongside the GWR line for three quarters of a mile before curving away past Cholsey Church towards Wallingford. From that date, as there was now a rail connection to the town, Wallingford Road station reverted to its original name of Moulsford.

More traffic needs more lines

Over time the railway carried more and more passengers and freight and therefore ran more and more, longer, and heavier trains. An issue which still dogs the railway network today is the disparate speeds of long-distance passenger, local passenger and freight trains. More lines were needed partly to segregate the slower trains from the expresses but more generally to provide flexibility. To this end additional land was obtained and additional tracks installed alongside the original lines. These new tracks eventually formed the *"Relief"* or *"Slow"* lines while the original road-bed became the *"Main"* or *"Fast"* line.

This work started from the London end, where traffic had become more dense, from 1873 with new four-track railway reaching Slough by mid-1879, and Taplow in 1884. Work on the section between Taplow and Didcot, started in mid-1890. Although some parts of the route were opened as temporary goods loops (where trains could be diverted off the main lines to allow other traffic to pass), the line was not opened throughout until 1899.

In the village the original road bridges, etc., were extended to the same design as originally, but slightly shorter in under-track length as the new standard gauge tracks required less space. These bridges all show evidence of this work as there are some visible differences in brickwork. Whilst the Gatehampton river crossing was treated similarly by extending the existing structure, the Moulsford crossing, as already mentioned, is built as a parallel structure in its own right but of matching design with slightly less embellishment.

In order to accommodate the new lines within the cutting beyond Moulsford station the existing parallel line of the Wallingford branch was truncated at a new station called Cholsey & Moulsford which was built in Cholsey at the point where the branch line curved away towards the northeast. The station at Moulsford itself was then closed and demolished.

This branch continued in operation until it ran its last passenger service in 1959, but freight, mainly to the ABM (Associated British Maltsters) malting, continued until 1981. The passenger service was known locally as the *"Bunk"*, though the origins of that name are obscure. There is a story that it originates because the one engine and one push-pull coach that operated the service somehow became uncoupled and the engine set off on its own, leaving the carriage and its passengers behind, thus *"doing a bunk"*!

The need for speed and associated developments

As already stated, Brunel's design was based on his intent that the GWR would be a high-speed railway and thus it has continued until today, mainly as a result of the development of locomotives and rolling stock, as well as improvements in the track and signalling, but still benefitting from Brunel's original level, sweeping, design.

Initial locomotives, specified by Brunel himself, were really totally inadequate and it was fortuitous that he employed Daniel Gooch as his locomotive superintendent in 1837. He soon got to grips with the issues and obtained some locos from the Stephensons – the first was *North Star* – followed by 11 more to the same design. He used these locos as the basis for further evolutionary designs such as the Firefly class used in the Gauge Commission trials, which easily attained 60mph. As well as pure speed the demands of increasing use of the railway meant that the locomotives needed to be capable of handling heavier and heavier loads, whilst maintaining the existing timetable. All of the over 100 initial locos were built under contract by other suppliers but, from 1846 onwards, all were built at their own new works constructed by the GWR at Swindon.

GWR locomotive designs continued to advance and by 1904 one of their locos *"City of Truro"*, had been reported to have achieved over 100mph, albeit descending an incline. By 1923 villagers would have been able to witness the daily passing of the Cheltenham Spa Express (popularly, though not officially, known as the Cheltenham Flyer) running from Swindon to Paddington in 75 minutes - an average of almost 62mph. By 1931 the timetable required an average of over 69mph and on a specially timed run an average of 81.6mph was obtained, whilst the regular daily service was further accelerated in September 1932 to require an average of 71.6mph. These are start to stop averages and thus the running speed here would have been well into the 80s. Quite a sight for local train spotters!

Those same spotters would have seen the experimental gas turbine locomotives that, though ordered by the GWR, were built and tested after the railway was nationalised in 1948, followed by diesels, which finally displaced steam, with trains now scheduled to run at up to 100mph. The next leap forward was the introduction into passenger service of the High Speed Train (HST) in 1976, capable of sustained 125mph running. This has now also passed into history locally and been replaced by bi-mode (25kV electric / diesel) Hitachi Intercity Express Trains (IETs) with their associated overhead masts and wires which have raised blood pressures and created a local group attempting to get the heavyweight design modified with structures more fitting, perhaps, to the location on the edge of an Area of Outstanding Natural Beauty (AONB).

As well as the express trains, both the GWR and its successors have also moved forward with local and goods train design and speeds. The GWR developed steam railcars or railmotors– self-propelled steam-driven passenger carriages – from 1903 and they remained in use until 1935. These were followed by streamlined diesel railcars from the 1930s to the early 1960s and both these types operated over the local railway lines. These were followed by Diesel Multiple Units replacing steam trains on local services in the British Rail, (BR) era, replaced by more modern ones – Class 165/166 Thames Turbos – in 1992, now also largely replaced by electric units, each one a step-change in acceleration and passenger facilities. At the same time goods trains have moved from transits at less than 30mph with brakes only on the loco and the trailing brake van to fully air-braked sets of wagons running at 75mph, with specialised wagons for specific commodities, including ISO (International Organisation for Standardisation) containers.

The Advanced Passenger Train (APT), using tilting technology to enable higher speeds on existing track, was developed by BR with a proposed service speed of 155mph (250kph), primarily for use on the Euston to Glasgow line which was, unlike the GWR, a line with many more, and tighter, curves. The initial gas turbine powered prototype made runs over the line here in 1975, attaining 152.3mph on a run from Swindon to Reading – a UK record – on 10th August that year.

In order to accommodate these advances the design, construction, and maintenance of the track itself has undergone significant changes. Rail technology advanced and, instead of Brunel's longitudinal baulks, track was laid on transverse wooden sleepers, held in *"chairs"* with wooden wedges which gradually evolved to what we now see. A heavy flat-bottom rail clipped to concrete or, sometimes, steel sleepers, and the rail welded continuously without "clickity-clack" joints. The advances in track technology are visible locally when work is done on the line. The complexity and capability of the machinery used is seen at close quarters, including relaying of continuous welded rail, ballast and sleeper replacement, rail grinding to maintain the correct rail profile, tamping to maintain levels, and high-speed track geometry monitoring.

Signalling

Initially trains were despatched on a time-interval basis without any communication between the origin and destination or intermediate locations. As the length of railway in operation increased staff (called Policemen) were installed to signal authority for trains to pass their position. They had *"boxes"* to allow them to shelter from the worst of the weather. These were rudimentary structures similar to a sentry box. They were also provided with mechanical signal apparatus – Brunel had designed a rotating head on a post such that it displayed a circular disc if the train could pass or a long transverse board if it had to stop. There was such a box on the village side of the Moulsford / Four Arches bridge in the initial years of operation. Their being defined as policemen led to the universal use, amongst railwaymen, of the term *"bobby"* to refer to any signalman, to this day.

The growth of traffic needed a more formal system and all railways started to install control systems that managed the traffic in what became known as block sections with signals admitting trains into each section under control of signal boxes. This system was enhanced by the installation of inter-box telegraph connections which formed the basis of signalling for the next hundred years.

The local area had quite long block sections (e.g. Goring to Cholsey) which limited the number of trains, particularly slow freight trains that could be moving through at any one time. Management did consider breaking up the blocks to effectively double the capacity but, until the heavy traffic requirements in the two World Wars, no action was taken.

Camouflaged Cross Keys pub with the signal box to the right by railway line

WW1 forced action and emergency intermediate block posts (signal boxes) were created – one at South Stoke in use from 1917 to 1920. WW2 saw a similar demand and a new box was installed here (on the embankment alongside the Cross Keys) in 1940 and this remained in use till 1953.

There are stories that enginemen on trains standing at the signals here in South Stoke would repair to the Cross Keys pub and leave a bucket which would be dislodged by the counterweight when the signal was cleared and the noise would summon them back to the footplate. This tale is repeated throughout the land wherever there is a pub adjacent to a signal but that is not to say that it is not true in the case of our village!

South Stoke signal box by the railway and next to the Cross Keys pub. Note the lettering on the pub denotes Simonds Brewery.

Technology and changes to traffic (e.g. closure of sidings at small stations) enabled control from remote centres and elimination of the traditional boxes, this area then being controlled from the Reading

Panel Box. It is now controlled from the Thames Valley Signalling Centre at Didcot, although most of the signal indications arise automatically from the passing of the trains themselves with the route setting for trains done by computer systems with human supervision rather than direct control except in emergencies. Proposed future systems (e.g. ERTMS = European Rail Traffic Management System) will eliminate fixed signals, replaced by in-cab displays plus advice to drivers as to the best speed to maintain.

Following an incident at Slough in 1906 where a driver passed danger signals and crashed, the GWR implemented a system (ATC - Automatic Train Control) which, through ramps installed in the middle of the track, advised the aspect of the associated signal to the driver by in-cab equipment and, if the signal was *"on"* would, if the driver did not acknowledge the warning, actually apply the brakes and bring the train to a stop. It was not until 1956, following the horrific Harrow & Wealdstone accident, that BR decided to introduce a similar system country-wide (AWS – Automatic Warning System). Following further accidents at Southall and Ladbroke Grove an extension to the system (TPWS - Train Protection & Warning System) was introduced with additional in-track and on-train kit which takes account of the train speed and applies the brakes to ensure the train will stop before the danger signal (or buffer stops in the case of terminal stations).

The "might have been" developments

Isaac King, the last lord of the manor and a tenant farmer of Christ Church, had sought to have the line diverted before it was built to avoid cutting through one of his meadows. He had written to his landlord as early as December 1834 regarding men measuring and surveying on his land for the purposes of building a railroad.

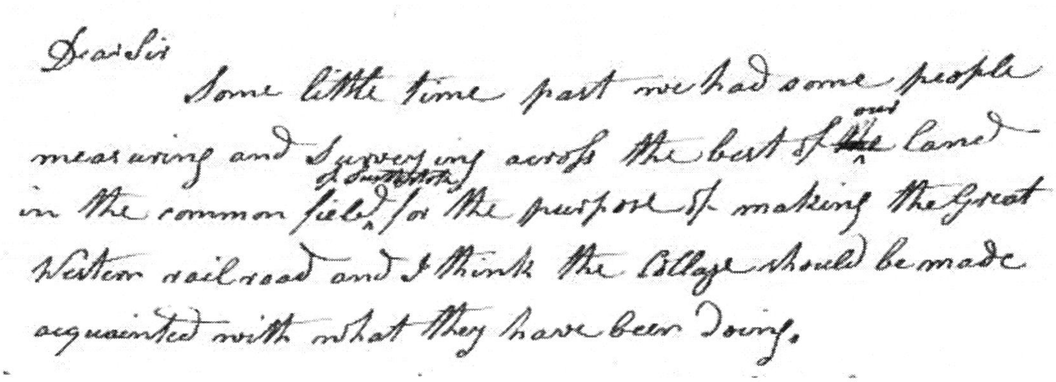
Dear Sir
Some little time past we had some people measuring and Surveying across the best of our land in the common field for the purpose of making the Great Western railroad and I think the College should be made acquainted with what they have been doing.

Were they aware of this and could they pass on to the appropriate party his objections? Three months later GWR tried to bribe Mr King by offering to *"build a proper Station house at Stoke...... upon the understanding that you will now withdraw the dissent..."* *(Christ Church Archives)*

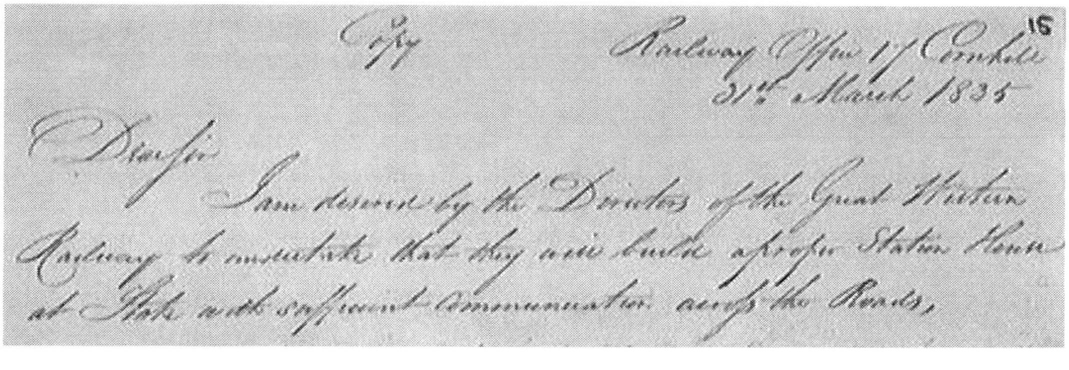
15
Copy
Railway Office 17 Cornhill
31st March 1835
Dear Sir
I am desired by the Directors of the Great Western Railway to [illegible] that they will build a proper Station House at Stoke with sufficient Communication across the Roads,

It is unlikely that there was ever any intent to deliver on this proposal as there would have been little originating traffic to make a station worthwhile.

Despite the proximity of Goring & Streatley station (2 miles away) it seems that there was an approach from the local Parish Council to the GWR in 1909, requesting that the village have its own station. The response was, as any sane person might have expected, that such a station was unlikely to generate a sufficient volume of traffic to warrant an additional station.

Similarly there was a request from local boat builder Sam Saunders for a railway siding to be built to enable materials for his Springfield Boat-building Works (now Withymead nature reserve) to be delivered direct. At the time goods had to be transferred at Goring to horse-drawn road transport. Some of these supplies, especially timber and mechanical equipment like boat engines would have been relatively heavy and cumbersome to transfer. It is difficult to envisage how such a connection could have been accomplished as it would have needed to be on the "fast" line side of the tracks and nothing came of it. Eventually Saunders left the area and relocated to the Isle of Wight forming the Saunders- Roe company building boats, aeroplanes and hovercraft.

SOURCES:

Specific references have not been noted in this document but the following sources have been used:-

"Isambard Kingdom Brunel" by L T C (Tom) Rolt ISBN 058210774X.

"Brunel's Didcot" by Jack Gardner ISBN 1870754 417.

"Brunel's Britain" by Derrick Beckett ISBN 07153 23601.

"Isambard Kingdom Brunel -The finest work in England" by David Clifford ISBN 1900467281 (This book is particularly useful if anyone wishes to read further on the construction of the railway which it examines in some detail, especially the contract (4R) for the section on the other side of Moulsford Bridge towards Didcot).

"Atlas of the Great Western Railway as at1947" by R A (Tony) Cooke ISBN 0 906867657 plus conversations with the author.

"The Pictorial Encyclopaedia of Railways" by Hamilton Ellis ISBN 0600375854.

"The Railway Navvies" by Terry Coleman ISBN 1784082325.

"From River to Sea: the Marine Heritage of Sam Saunders" by Ray Wheeler ISBN 1873295057.

Items extracted from local newspaper archives and other sources by past and present members of the South Stoke Historical Society, and held in its collections.

Archives of the Worcester Locomotive Society.

South Oxfordshire District Council Planning Portal online where Application P98/W0250/LB contains plans and many photographs of the internal structure of Moulsford Bridge prior to repair and waterproofing work.

Junction of Ferry Road with The Street looking south. Behind the wall on the left is Manor Farm and the church beyond. On the right is Frewin's Close

CHAPTER11

SOUTH STOKE – ROADS AND BYWAYS

The village of South Stoke is an ancient one, situated on the east bank of the Thames between Goring and Crowmarsh with its main thoroughfare, The Street, running parallel to the river some 330 yards (c.302m) away across the water meadows. The Victoria County History records South Stoke as: *"situated on rather marshy meadow bordering the river"*, and also flourishing throughout the Middle Ages on account of its *"farming, fishery, (wind)mill and woods"*.

The riverbank itself is 142ft (43m) above sea level with the level of the river being normally 2 ft (0.6m) below the bank. The altitude of The Street is 146ft (44.5m) and the Church (set on high ground beside it) is 153ft (46.6m). The land rises to 170ft (52m) at the B4009 (Wallingford Road), then continues to rise steadily towards Woodcote with White Hill on the left being 281ft (85.6m) high and Catsbrain Hill on the right 248ft (75.6m). St Leonard's Church at Woodcote is 511ft (156m) above sea level.

The land between the village and the river is clearly low-lying and subject to periodic flooding. It consists of water meadows bounded by drainage ditches. The land on the eastern side of the Wallingford Road (B4009) has always been good agricultural land and for centuries to the present day has been intensively farmed on a crop rotation basis. This land is now known locally as *"The Prairie"* on account of its immense field landscape and lack of hedges.

White Hill as seen from the Woodcote Road. Above, harvesting in the 1950s. Below, a barley field today.

There is evidence of prehistoric settlement in the area dating back as far as 3,000 BC. Even then it was rich farming land; whilst the adjacent river provided water, fish, transportation and protection for the inhabitants. Stone Age, Bronze and Iron Age people all made use of it. North Stoke especially, is rich in archaeological sites of that period; but South Stoke also has its polygonal enclosures, burial pits, linear features and circles. These are in two main areas: between Freedom Cottages and "*the Oaks*", extending up White Hill; and from Watch Folly Hill running down to Kaffir Farm on the east and to Ivol Barn on the south. In the latter area especially are several burial pits. Close by is a section of what once was the Icknield Way, a major old road and certainly pre-Roman connecting what is now East Anglia with the west of England.

The road connecting South Stoke with Wallingford and Goring was known in earlier times as the Tidgsing Way or Tuddingway, and dates from the 13th century: this is now the B4009. Within the village itself the main thoroughfare was the north/south Street, which at one time continued south along the present bridleway towards Cleeve (and the nearest watermill) but swung east to Grove Farm. This is now styled The Ridgeway, one of the designated National Trails.

The following map is based upon the information in the Eynsham Cartulary Vol. II showing the roads through the village and beyond around 1366. The broken lines indicate that these paths/roads no longer exist though they were still thoroughfares up to the mid-19th century. The dotted line North-South through the village itself disappeared under the railway embankment c.1838-1840. The others remained until the Enclosures of 1853.

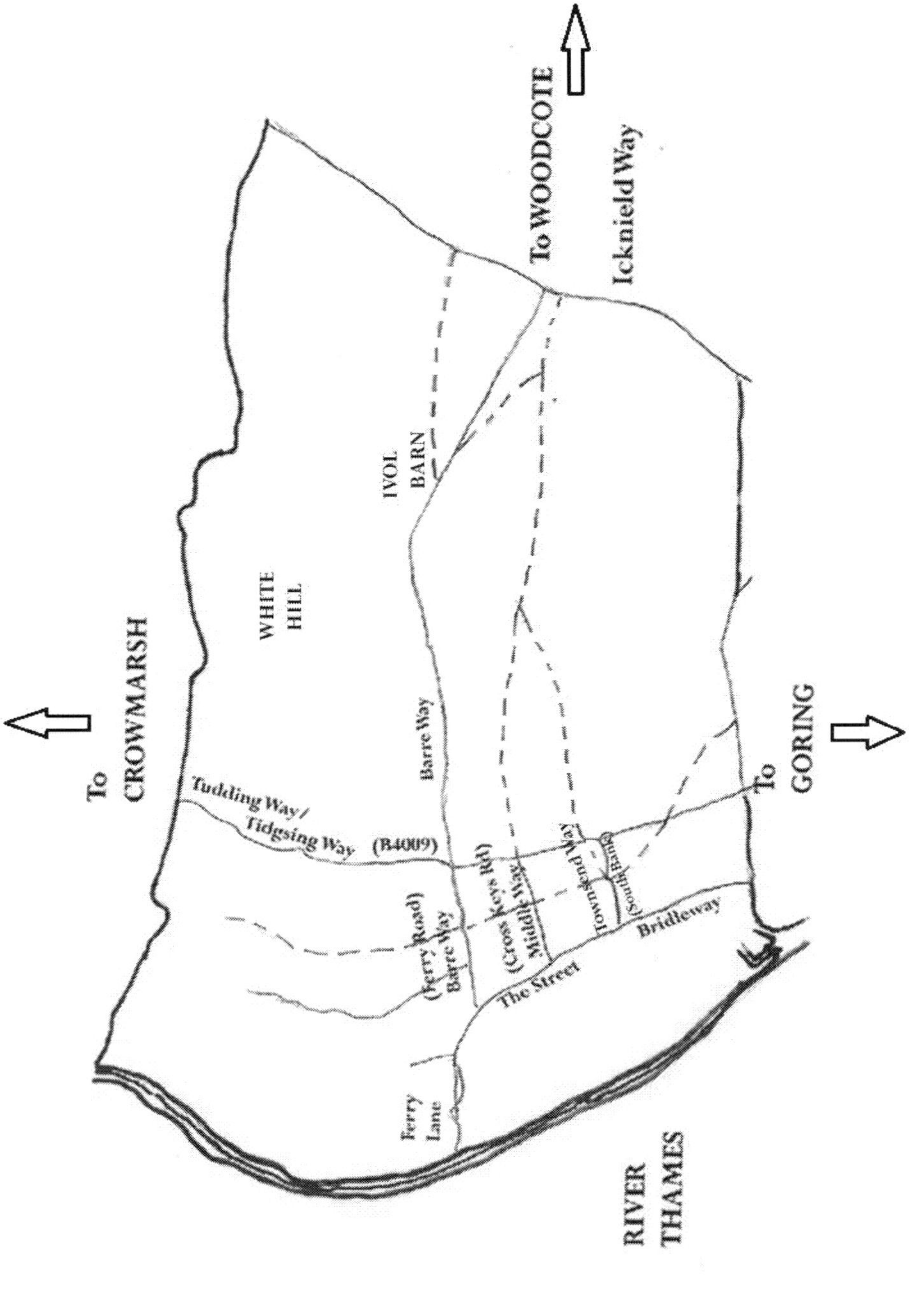

South Stoke's road system from 1366 to the present

A short footpath running parallel to The Street between the Church and Stoke Abbas house was formerly known as Churchway but is now called the Bierpath. This path is so named as it was the route used for the conveyance of coffins on a type of handcart called a *"bier"* to the church and churchyard. East of this path was a track running along the line of the present railway which served the fields to the north and south of the village. A map in the Archives at Christ Church, Oxford, shows the two paths and the road layout in and around the village in 1818. The Bierpath continued through what is now Chapel Close and Deacon Field.

The 14th century Barre Way is today the east to west road from Woodcote to South Stoke, crossing the B4009 and into the village at Ferry Road. The Barre Way was named after William de la Barre who was granted a *"messuage"* (a dwelling house with outbuildings and land assigned to its use) in South Stoke by Eynsham Abbey, as is recorded in the Eynsham Cartulary of 1264 (see Appendix 1). Parallel to this ran the medieval Middle and Townsend Ways (the present Cross Keys and South Bank roads), both of which once extended across the Wallingford Road to join up with the Barre Way. But both these extensions were removed at the time of the 1853 Enclosures, as were the old Burying Way and Deans Way which once connected with the Icknield Way.

The Roman occupation of AD 43-407 saw the establishment of a main settlement in Dorchester and a smaller one at Benson. However, the area south of Benson was not to benefit from the network of hard Roman roads built north of Dorchester. Accordingly for centuries the South Oxfordshire area had to make do with its primitive system of rough, unmaintained tracks "*full of potholes, worn into ruts by cartwheels, muddy in wet weather, dusty in dry*".

Although in the 16th century parishes were made responsible for the upkeep of their roads, with Surveyors of Highways being appointed by parishioners, nonetheless villagers had to provide materials, carts and horses as well as their own labour so in consequence a good road system never really materialised. However, a first available record, which shows that the Vestry of South Stoke was by then dealing with the maintenance of its roads, in addition to Church affairs, law and order and the poor, is an Account Book of 1766. In this book the Supervisor of Highways, one William Markes, has recorded for that year a total rate collected locally (at one penny in the pound) of £3-8-0, of which expenditure was £2-3-2, leaving a balance of £1-4-10. The main items of expenditure were £1-4-0 for "*the picking of stones*" and 11/6d for "*beare for the labores on the High Way*". A year later the beer provided for the labourers amounted to 10/6d, and only 10/8d was spent on "*picking 32 loads of stones*". In subsequent years however, total expenditure on the roads was to rise to £9-14-4, and by 1791 had virtually doubled to £20. There are only two such Account Books available in the parish records, the one dating from 1766-1794 and the other from 1842-1845.

The labourers were initially rewarded by beer but were later paid around one shilling (5p) for a day's work. The work of picking up stones appears as the most frequent accounting entry. This task seems mainly to have been done by women during the winter months, with stones being collected from the nearby fields. During the winter some five or six labourers were employed, falling to two or three in the summer. In 1843 up to 15 men were employed between January and March to repair flood damage to the roads. Later disbursements included the hire of carts and horses for

The Street at the southern end of the village looking north. Early 1900s

Further along The Street looking south, with the old Plough & Harrow on the left and the Vicarage wall on the right

collecting gravel and sums were paid to carpenters, wheelers and blacksmiths for their services.

The 18th century saw the coming of turnpike roads which were taken out of parish control and placed in the hands of trustees. In 1763 one such road (the present A329) was built from Shillingford Bridge to Reading, on the Berkshire rather than the Oxfordshire side of the river. South Stoke and the surrounding area had to await the 1894 Local Government Act which put control of the highways under the Rural District Council, before any real improvements were made locally. Heavy building materials, bricks, roof tiles, timbers etc. had to be laboriously hauled from Goring Station by horse and cart along the rutted and muddy unsealed road to South Stoke. Oxford County Council Highways surfaced the now B4009 in the early 20th century thus making it suitable for the new motor traffic which was steadily increasing.

SOURCES:

Victoria County History, Oxfordshire Vol 7 originally published 1962.

Steve Ford- two papers on Settlement Patterns around North and South Stoke and Mary Jessop *"History of Oxfordshire"* (Phillimore and Co 1975).

Bullock family scrapbook.

PAR254/5/F1/3 The Overseers of Poor Accounts, 1779-1790 can be seen in the Oxfordshire Heritage Centre

CHAPTER 12

SOUTH STOKE AND THE RIVER THAMES

The river has always played an important part in the lives of the South Stoke inhabitants, providing fish, raw materials, transport and recreation. Eels, important in Medieval times, were caught in eel grigs (traps) made of withy reeds (the long flexible shoots of the osier willow), or eel bucks made of willow rods, set in wooden frames and located at the bottom of the river. The beds along the South Stoke stretch of river provided willow rods used for local industries such as hurdle-making and fencing and the withies were useful in basket weaving.

The osier willow and withy beds could pose quite a hazard to those towing boats or barges upstream, as was explained by John Bickerdyke in his "*Thames Rights and Thames Wrongs*" of 1895, "*Towing is a favourite method of proceeding upstream by persons in small boats. Just above Moulsford ferry* (at South Stoke) *a withy bed is planted by the side of the river, on its very edge. The towpath is supposed to skirt the withies. Barges usually attempt to drag their lines over the bed, but I have frequently seen their towropes caught in the fences, and troublesome delays have been occasioned. But in the case of small boats, the passing of the towing line over this withy bed is a matter of considerable difficulty and danger*".

South Stoke's nearest market town was, and still is, Wallingford. Once the first stone bridge was built to cross the Thames in the reign of Henry III (1216-1272) it became an important trading centre serving the surrounding villages in the Thames Valley. During the 15th century the town's people suffered a dip in trade but with wool and malt becoming important commodities their fortunes revived and the river movement of these goods increased.

In the late 16th century a number of weirs were constructed along the Thames to assist river traffic, and by 1790 modern-style pound locks had replaced flash locks at Benson, Cleeve and Goring. By then a great network of canals was being constructed to serve the industrial Midlands and to connect the Thames Valley with the north. Barge traffic carrying goods was increasing rapidly and in 1751 a body known as the Thames Commissioners was set up to control navigation. This was in turn replaced in 1857 by the Thames Conservancy and modern locks were built, at Benson in 1870, Cleeve in 1874 and at Goring in 1922.

Wallingford now became a major centre for the new barge traffic and by the end of the 18th century some 8,000 tons of cargo was being landed annually at its wharf, with a further 12,000 tons passing up and downstream to other destinations. The towpath from Wallingford ran down the Berkshire bank of the river as far as Little Stoke where the horses that towed the barges would cross over to the Oxfordshire bank by a flat type ferry which was usually poled across. The horses were carried across two at a time. Originally the towpath went straight down to Cleeve from South Stoke but was later to re-cross the river by ferry at South Stoke, continuing along the Berkshire bank down to Streatley. The Beetle and Wedge is on the Berkshire bank and that property owned the ferry operation. Passengers summoned the ferryman originally by means of a horn. Sheep would also cross here from South Stoke to Moulsford for dipping.

1897 looking across the river to The Beetle and Wedge

The opposite bank still slopes into the river but the hotel is now extended

Mid-C20th, opposite bank is reinforced. Note ferry calling bell on post

The Beetle and Wedge today

Up to the Second World War the river was a very busy place with many horse-drawn barges carrying timber, grain, iron, coal, pottery, bricks and stone as well as machinery of all types. Fertilizer and bulk materials arrived at South Stoke by barge and were unloaded at the bottom of Ferry Lane. There was no landing stage but planks would be laid out so that farm carts could back up to the moored barge.

Wheat from South Stoke was transported by barge downstream to the water-powered mill at Streatley. After threshing, the grain would be taken by horse and cart down Ferry Lane to the riverbank (now the site of the slipway, constructed in 2000 to mark The Millennium) where it was loaded onto the transporter's horse-drawn barge. The horse would then cross the river to the Moulsford bank on a flatboard alongside the barge. Threshed barley from South Stoke would go by barge to Wallingford, or even Abingdon, to be used in beer making. The horses used were Welsh Cobs – very strong, fast and sure-footed in sticky and muddy conditions. The horses worked in pairs but, if the work was hard, sometimes in triples.

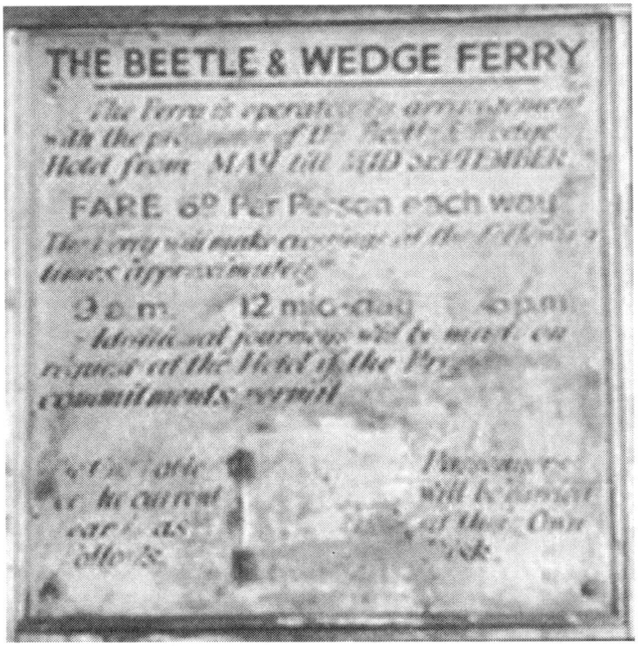

By the early 1960s the ferry service had become uneconomical and was discontinued but, above is a poor photograph taken in 1980 of the old notice board when it was still in situ by the river crossing. It has long since been removed.

From 1887 the Goring and Streatley Regatta was an annual event until 1914. It was held on August Bank Holiday Saturday and was one of the biggest regattas on the river with special train services from Paddington and reports appearing in the London daily newspapers. Many famous clubs competed and the course was from the Beetle and Wedge at Moulsford to Cleeve Lock. Houseboats, punts and rowing boats lined the course and marquees were erected along the riverbank. The regatta was successfully revived in 1993 and is still held (2020).

In 1830 Moses Saunders started a business in Streatley at The Swan boathouse originally concerned with weir and lock construction but was later to concentrate on boat building. In 1890 his two grandsons expanded the business with Samuel taking over the Goring wharf for boat building and his brother, Arthur, managing the remaining business at The Swan. Both now concentrated on building steam launches and other river craft and became renowned for their lightweight *"sewn"* mahogany hulls. One of the boats which still remains in use is called *"Consuta"* after the Latin word, consuta, which means sewn.

In 1897 Samuel Saunders moved his Springfield Works to an inlet on the Goring/South Stoke parish boundary. Here he expanded his boat building and employed young men from South Stoke until after the First World War when the Works were closed. Samuel Saunders then moved his business to Cowes where the firm became Saunders Roe in 1929. The firm later became British Hovercraft. Remnants of the Saunders slipways and sheds are now within the Withymead Nature Reserve and can be seen on the Reserve's open days.

The village had a swimming club further up the river, on the South Stoke bank, from the Second World War to 1965. Part of the riverbank was netted and diving boards were constructed. This was also where, from the 1930s, the school children were taught to swim.

Club members in the 1930s. Note the specially designed badges

The scene from the site of the Swimming Club today

The village still has an active Angling Club with fishing rights as far as the Four Arches Bridge. A London club used to regularly bring a coach load of fishermen down at weekends during the season. The Perch and Pike pub recorded catches, and at one time the pub landlord was the water bailiff and there were pike and perch exhibited in glass cases.

The brick railway bridge over the river, upstream from South Stoke has been known locally since its construction as the *"Four Arches Bridge"*. It is a listed building. It was built between 1838 and 1840 and is described as *"the Moulsford Railway Viaduct by I. K. Brunel....of red brick with stone dressings....four elliptical arches with stone surrounds and brick parapet"*. This bridge carries the main line from Paddington to the west.

Beside the Four Arches Bridge, on both sides of the river, are pillboxes dating from the Second World War. The one on the South Stoke side of the river is of brick rather than concrete, the usual building material. These pillboxes were built all along the Thames to guard against a possible German invasion. On the Oxfordshire bank the next pillbox upstream is at Little Stoke overlooking the old ferry crossing. There used to be a pillbox at the South Stoke ferry, but it has long since been demolished. Downstream there were two pillboxes on high ground near the Leatherne Bottel.

At the Leatherne Bottel was the *"celebrated Cleeve Spring"* where visitors used to fill their leather bottles with the spring water. In the South Stoke Village Survey of 1941-42 this spring was recorded as having *"a considerable reputation for its healing properties"*.

Another spring fed one of the three ponds in the village, located in the yard of Manor Farm, (see page 187). In 1941 an old inhabitant recounted a story told to him by his father about this spring: *"When the pond was cleaned out"* he said, *"a streak of water shot up in the middle of the pond no thicker than my finger"*. Today the pond is no longer in existence; it was filled in many years ago, but its site can still be seen in the low-lying ground within the confines of the Manor Farm yard wall, just opposite the house called Frewins' Close. Another pond was Barre Pond which gave its name to the cottages behind, on the footpath to Little Stoke, and also to the more recent house beside Ferry Road, now known as November Cottage. Yet another pond was once alongside Fulbrook House. Both these ponds have long since been filled in.

Parts of Manor Farm date from when South Stoke was in the ownership of Eynsham Abbey. Fish supplemented a Benedictine monk's diet and a regular supply was ensured by constructing a series of fishponds, in the area bounded by the track to Little Stoke on the east, Ferry Road to the south, and the line of cottages from the "Granary" to "Fishponds" house on the west. These fishponds were extremely low-lying, being only a few feet above the river and being fed by drainage ditches and run-off from those three sides. They were connected to the river by a main ditch flowing west out of the northern end of the fishponds area, which then swung south to cross Ferry Lane before joining the river at a point opposite to Moulsford's Ferry Lane. It is not known exactly how many fishponds there were in medieval times but, so legend has it, they were possibly tended by one or two monks who lived in a tiny cottage, which became incorporated into "Fishponds" house as its old dining room. Some five fishponds are clearly recognisable in what is now a densely wooded and overgrown area of some 12 acres. This was once open marsh and meadow land, with clumps of trees here and there. The area is still an important drainage area for the village as a whole.

The low-lying situation of South Stoke has in the past led to flooding and of particular note was "*the great flood of 1947*", which flooded the length of the village street. However, by the early 1990s operation of all the weir gates on the Thames were linked by computer, thus reducing the likelihood of future flooding. There have also been improvements in the drainage system in the village and the clearing out of drainage ditches.

Corner House at the junction of The Street & Ferry Lane, flooded in 1947

College farmyard just round the corner from Corner House in 1947

SOURCES:

Victoria County History, Oxfordshire Vol 7 originally published 1962.

Steve Ford- two papers on Settlement Patterns around North and South Stoke and Mary Jessop *"History of Oxfordshire"* (Phillimore and Co 1975).

Bullock family scrapbook.

John Leyland *"The Thames Illustrated"* 1901.

John Bickerdyke *"Thames Rights and Wrongs"* 1895.This author was a resident in the parish of South Stoke and one time editor of The Fisherman's Gazette.

Ferry Lane looking north, above pre-1905, below today

Ferry Lane looking south, before the 1905 fire. Below the same view today. The thatched properties on the right were all consumed in the fire

CHAPTER 13

THE GREAT FIRE OF SOUTH STOKE 1905

The Great Fire of South Stoke in 1905 is the stuff of legends in village folklore but, as we shall see, there is more to the story than the terrible events in August of that year, as it was not the only major conflagration to hit the village in years past. But, let's not get ahead of ourselves: we should start with the 1905 fire as it is very well documented. The account which follows originally came from the contributors to the Happy Circle Book in the early 1960s and at that time there may well have been villagers who could remember the actual fire. In their youth it would have made a big impression on them. Appendix 4 reproduces an example of a contemporary news report from the Berks and Oxon Advertiser.

August 1905

Before the introduction of combine harvesters in the late 1950s all cut cereal crops were stacked in stooks to dry in the fields. They were then stored in ricks during the winter or until such time as needed.

Rick fires were very common indeed as a result of sparks from chimneys and bonfires. Villages such as South Stoke, with a railway line nearby, were particularly at risk from sparks from the steam locomotives. In living memory, the fields between the B4009 road and the railway would regularly catch fire as a result of train sparks.

The rickyard behind the Corner House where the fire started, see map

On Saturday 19th August, 1905[1] a very strong wind was blowing (almost a gale) when Reginald Strange, a boy of six whose father was a shepherd, was playing with matches and set fire to some loose straw in Mr. Brock's farm yard not far from Waises Cottage.[2] Within half-an-hour some 20 ricks and a number of thatched farm buildings were ablaze.

Fanned by the strong wind, the inferno spread rapidly along Ferry Road destroying several farm buildings and cottages, all of which had straw thatched roofs. The Wallingford Fire Brigade was contacted by telegram at 4.30 pm and their new steam fire engine under the direction of Captain W. Honeybone was on the scene within the hour, followed by the smaller manual engines from Pangbourne, Whitchurch, Goring and Reading.

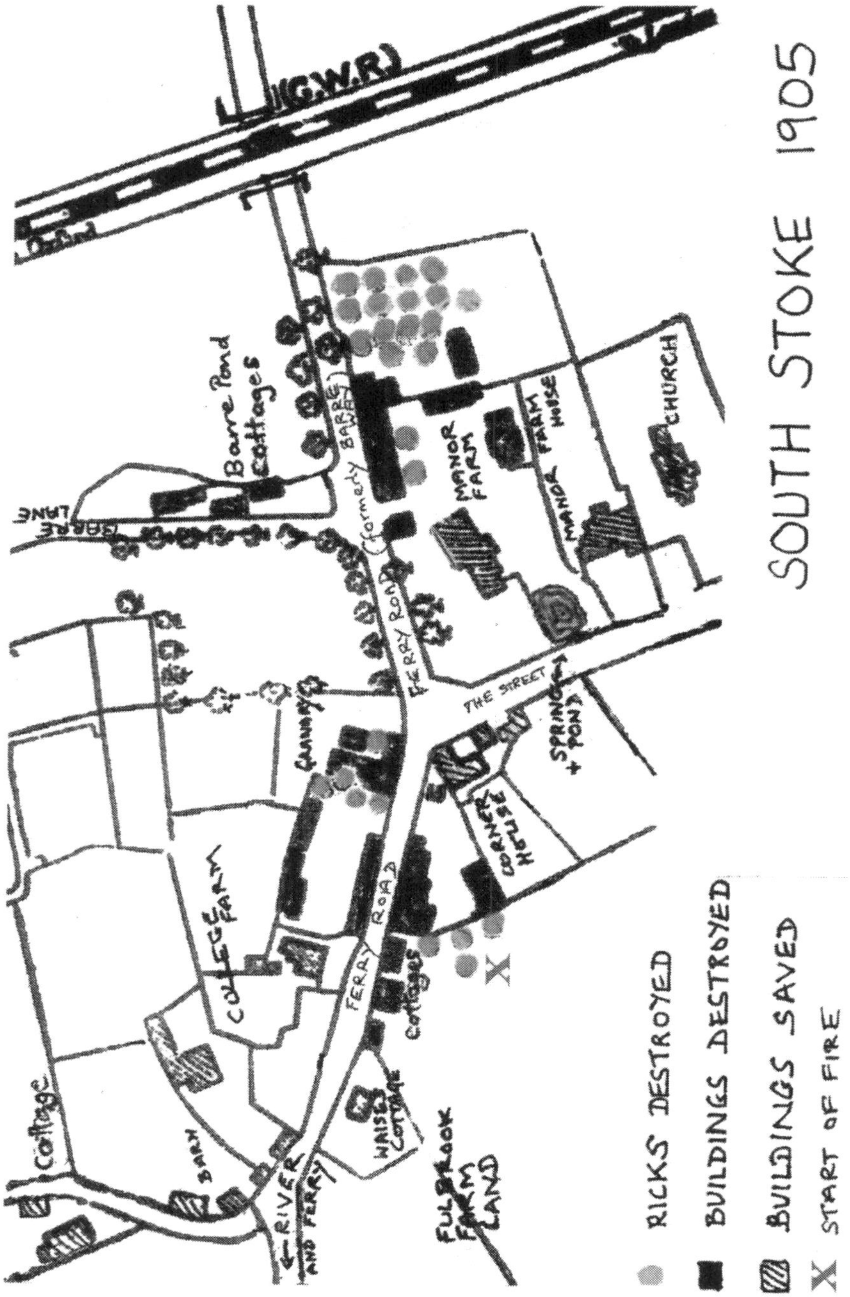

Map showing the source and spread of the fire in 1905 (Oxford Times)

The flames crossed Ferry Road to College Farm where several outbuildings and stables were destroyed, though College Farm House was saved. The fire spread further along Ferry Road destroying the granary, a number of ricks, a barn full of unthreshed barley, stabling, a cowshed and two cart sheds – all part of College Farm which in 1872 had been amalgamated with Manor Farm under the tenancy of brothers George and John Bullock.

Wreckage in College farm yard after the fire. Across the road are the gables of the Corner House then a farm.

On the opposite side of Ferry Road all barns and buildings were destroyed between Waises Cottage and The Corner House. With a change of wind direction, burning straw from these buildings was carried up Ferry Road from the junction with The Street, setting alight two thatched cottages opposite the entrance to Manor Farm. [Manor Farm is now called *"Manor House"*] These cottages were owned by the Parish Council and were lived in by two elderly people, Edward Kew and Mary White, and were completely destroyed though some furniture and belongings were saved.

Burning debris blown across the road set fire to a large barn belonging to Manor Farm and some ricks and other buildings were destroyed. But The Dovecote and Manor Farm House escaped the flames, as did the Church. A great deal of agricultural machinery was destroyed as were two barns containing threshed wheat, barley and oats. However, in spite of the speed and intensity of the fire no-one was injured and not a single head of livestock was lost.

Atmospheric photo of the fire in progress at Manor Farm

A completely demolished barn and farm implements in the foreground at Manor Farm. In the background the coach house (seen in previous photo) which had all its doors and windows burnt.

Being summer, the spring and pond at Manor Farm[3] were running low but under the command of Captain Honeybone hoses were joined together to reach the Thames enabling the new Wallingford steam fire engine to pump water from the river to the pond. Using the manual fire engines water was then pumped by hand from the pond to wherever it was needed. The Fire Brigades were in attendance all that night and until midday on the Sunday but on Monday morning (21st August) some of the rick remains and charred beams from the cottages were still smouldering.

The pond at Manor farm (since filled in) showing two manual fire engines

In all 27 ricks were destroyed and, with the exception of Moss Cottage (then a timbered and thatched single storey cottage), the entire west end of South Stoke's barns, cottages and outbuildings were obliterated from Waises to the Ferry Road railway bridge. The only remaining buildings were College Farm House, The Corner House and, further east, Manor Farm House and its Dovecote.

Carried by the gale, burning debris from the fire was found as far away as seven miles from South Stoke and in the week following the fire over 1,000 sightseers descended on the village to view the devastation, crossing the river by ferry from Moulsford.

After the fire College Farm on the far right still remains but a chimney on the left is all that remains of the Fulbrook's thatched property

Young men stood by the side of the remains of the chimney

After the fire

A great deal of building materials were needed to rebuild the devastated village. In the water meadows (behind Ashmount House) a drainage ditch leading down to the river was enlarged. Bricks, timber, sand and cement were brought by boat along the Thames and then floated up this cutting through the meadows to Ferry Road. The red brick barns and walls bear witness to the rebuilding of this end of South Stoke.

Later in 1905

On Thursday, 4th September, only two weeks after the terrifying inferno of 19th August which threatened the lives and homes of the whole of South Stoke, another fire broke out. This time, in a barn at the other end of the village belonging to Mr. T.P. Hatt, behind the Chapel and within a few feet of "Elmlea", now known as "The Malthouse".

The barn and its contents of barley were destroyed but the fire was contained and Elmlea, the Chapel and a number of cottages and furniture were saved. Once again, the Wallingford steam fire engine was in attendance and with help from the Whitchurch and Goring Brigades hoses were joined together in order to obtain water from the river. The Wallingford Fire Brigade remained at the site until the next morning. This fire was thought to have been started deliberately.

The following weekend, another fire broke out about a mile from South Stoke, this time at Mr. Guy's farm at Springfield. A rick of hay was completely destroyed and again it was thought to have been started deliberately. A reward of £25 was offered for the conviction of the arsonists.

1907

In 1907, The Berkshire Chronicle reported on two fires in South Stoke in their editions of Saturday, 12th January and Saturday, 19th January.

The first fire, believed to have been started deliberately, broke out in Mr. Bullock's Manor Farm yard when late in the evening of Sunday, 6th January a wheat rick was seen to be fully alight. Appearing to be a case of arson, P.C. Snellgrove at Goring Police Station was informed at midnight and he immediately started out for South Stoke.

The Wallingford Fire Brigade was contacted but they declined to attend. However, the Pangbourne Brigade arrived soon after 2.00 am on the Monday morning with their new steam fire engine and firemen were able to fully contain the fire.

In the meantime, before the arrival of the Brigade, Mr. Bullock and helpers had spread wetted sheets around the burning rick in an attempt to prevent the fire from spreading. Eventually this particular rick was completely destroyed but the Pangbourne firemen remained on duty all through the night until 9.00 am the following morning dowsing the charred remains until there was no danger to farm buildings and other ricks. This was the first time Pangbourne's new steam fire engine had been called out.

On the following Saturday evening between 11.00 pm and midnight there was another presumed arson attack in South Stoke. This time at Mr. T.P. Hatt's farm, which was in the centre of the village. Mr. G. Druce discovered a hay rick in flames and with help managed to cut away the burning corner of the rick, preventing the fire from spreading to other ricks close by and endangering sheep and lambs penned within the farmyard. As this appeared to be another arson attack P.C. Rowse, at Goring Police Station, was sent for to investigate the matter.

1868 and 1873

As indicated in the introduction to this chapter, the events of 1905 were preceded by earlier incidents which, although not reported publically in such detail, were nonetheless quite serious in their effect. Perhaps the worst of these incidents was the fire which broke out in early July 1868. At about midday a "serious fire" occurred reducing "to ashes" an old farmhouse and five cottages. Four of the properties belonged to a young farmer who worked 400 acres – Mr. Hatt and the other two to Mr. Marshall, "late of Cholsey". The poor cottagers were rendered homeless and nearly all lost their belongings but some, the newspaper states, were "kindly offered shelter". However, in an agricultural area the homes were not the only casualties. "Two ricks of hay and four stacks of straw, and 50 quarters of thrashed oats, two barns, a threshing machine, ploughs (and) harrows" were destroyed and all caused, it was thought, by children playing with matches.[4]

Nearly five years later in 1873, a fire broke out of a very "alarming and destructive nature" that could be seen for "many miles round". The Wallingford fire engine was soon in attendance though the villagers, men and women, were doing their utmost to protect adjacent thatched cottages from the flames. It was thought the fire had originated "from some hot wood ashes being placed near some farm buildings". Three barns, some stables, outbuildings, two ricks, a large quantity of straw and two cottages "were alight by the time the villagers were aroused". Great difficulty was experienced in getting out the livestock. "The horses were all saved, and some fat hogs were carried out on stretchers. Five pigs however were burnt to death". A thousand pounds worth of damage was done that evening to the property of Mr. R P King, the largest farmer in the area, again to the unfortunate Mr. Hatt, Mr. Bosher and the two cottagers who luckily were insured.[5]

ENDNOTES:

1. 15th September 1905, Berks. & Oxon. Advertiser. 19th September 1905, The Berkshire Chronicle.

2. Mr. Brock lived at The Elms, a large house (now demolished) in Ferry Road on the far side of the railway bridge. A number of modern bungalows now stand on the site. Mr. Brock farmed the land of Fulbrook Farm, but Fulbrook House itself was separately rented out by Christ Church.

3. The spring and pond at Manor Farm disappeared in the very hot summer of 1947 when it dried out completely. It was filled in with general rubbish, grassed over and Martin Bullock's father (Frank) planted the apple trees seen today.

4. 11th and 18th July 1868, The Reading Mercury.

5. 3rd May 1873, The Reading Mercury, Oxford Gazette, Newbury Herald and Berkshire County Paper.

Accounts from Martin Bullock and the late Byron Alexander.

Ferry Lane looking south showing College Farm on the left. On the right the low barn was rebuilt in the early decades of the 20th century.

The middle of The Street northward then and now. Kate's Cottage, right

CHAPTER 14

EDUCATION IN SOUTH STOKE

For centuries the Church was the sole body providing a rudimentary form of education at village level. During the 17th century more schools were set up than in the previous 100 years, but the impetus was still of a religious nature. Dr. Griffith Higgs, an eminent Churchman and distinguished citizen of South Stoke who died in 1659, left an endowment of £600 to buy land in the parish, from which he hoped a sufficient annual income would be realised to enable a charity school to be set up and maintained in the village for at least eight poor children. At the same time, on a national basis, the Movement for Charity Schools that had begun early in the 18th century was followed around 1780 by the Sunday School Movement; with both being concerned to provide primary education to the poor and needy.

Detail of Dr Griffith Higgs' Memorial

At South Stoke it seems that throughout the 18th century Dr. Higgs' bequest was providing some £5 a year for the education of children in the village; possibly being conducted in the Church or vicarage, since no specific building was in existence at that time. Such income had by 1808 risen to £15 a year, when "*some seven poor children were being taught to read*".[1] More information about the Higgs' bequest is given in a Glebe Terrier of 1806 that mentions the local school, "*for the endowment of which Dr. Higgs left £600 to be laid out in purchasing lands; this land consists of 22 and a half acres, is situated in the common fields of South Stoke and is at present let for the sum of 10 guineas*".

At the base of the Higgs' Memorial - a constant reminder of his legacy

By 1818 the rent was still only bringing in £15 and this was used to pay Mr Edward Edwards, the then master of the school. Local testimony to government Commissioners looking into the education of the poor in 1818 explained that there was no school house in South Stoke and that the curate Rev. Mill had never seen any deeds regarding Higgs and the £600 that was meant to provide for a school. Dependent on how much rent could be raised (on what was supposedly bad land) the master's free school places varied from 6 to 10. In 1818 there were some ten pupils, all boys, with some additional paying pupils. It seems the boys were very young when they started school because when *"parents want their (the boys') work, they are taken away from the school"* but there were always others admitted. The school was *"always kept full" however* education at this time was rudimentary to say the least. The boys were only taught to read and nothing more. If there ever were any spare places then girls could attend and as well as learning to read they would be taught how to knit by the master's wife. The master had been well qualified to teach but in 1818 he was very old and worse, had been blind for some 3 or 4 years! His wife appears to have tried to help with the teaching but not very successfully and consequently the children were *"remiss in their attendance"* and the school *"very ill conducted"*. [2]

Further information appears in the Burials Register of 1813-1903, where there is a note by Philip Nind (who was vicar from 1844 to 1886) to the effect that "*the utmost I can obtain from the school land is £24 per annum*". A further note in the Churchwardens' Accounts for 1863 to 1893 says that "*it is quite clear the present acreage does not come up to that which £600 would have represented some 200 years ago*". All this would seem to support the allegation that a nephew of Dr. Griffith Higgs, who was the executor of the Doctor's estate, betrayed his trust and misappropriated part of the £600 that was meant to have been spent on the purchase of land. Indeed the nephew seems in later life to have repented of what he had done, and asked not to be buried inside the Church alongside other members of his family, but to lie outside instead. The inscription above the church porch reads in part: "... *in it I feared within the Church to be interred. But meekly I my God implore, a place to lye tho' at the door*". In 1837 the Estate Diaries of Christ Church record responses to a census that they had undertaken, part (VII) of which related to Parochial Schools. It was stated that there were two schools in the parish, one in Woodcote erected in 1720 and the other in South Stoke itself. This was allegedly erected in 1830. It is uncertain whether the Charity (Free) School had a permanent site in South Stoke. Indeed, Note 2 in how to fill out a return for the parliamentary Education Commission for the years 1853-57 states that *"a school meant a distinct group of scholars under the instruction of a headmaster or headmistress and NOT a separate school building"*. Rev. Philip Nind, Vicar of the Parish, was later to record: *"I have never been able to ascertain that any classroom ever existed here (before 1840)... when one was built, chiefly at the expense of the Patrons of the Living, which was pulled down when the present school was built (in 1862) and the site changed..."*. An Estate map of South Stoke Rectory Farm dated 1853, (though it could be a copy of an earlier map) shows a small school site on the north side of the building that is currently known as The White House on The Street in the centre of the village. The map has references showing the site of what was to become the school as *"House and Garden"*. This source is a conundrum for by 1853 the school was located next to the church. The map may have been used primarily to show land held by Rectory Farm but still showing a prior use of village properties, thus solving the puzzle. The Christ Church census continues to record that both schools in the parish were in a deplorable state and financial support was lacking the costs falling primarily upon the reluctant clergy. As an agricultural village the church thought of the population as being *"of low moral condition"*. Many of its farmers being nonconformists were indifferent or hostile to church matters. Isaac King, the largest tenant farmer at this time was instrumental in a Chapel being built in South Stoke in 1820 at a time when no vicar was living within the village so why would these farmers wish to assist in supporting a school influenced by a Church of England?

In the early years of the 19th century, primary education in general was largely in the hands of two main societies working to improve educational facilities in the country. They were doing much to get new schools built, but were still far from meeting the needs of the nation. These societies were known as The British and Foreign Schools' Society, and the National Society for Promoting the Education of the Poor in the Principles of the Established Church (a Church of England organisation). It appears this latter Society helped financially with whatever school there was in South Stoke in 1837 along with The Treasury. By 1833 the government had begun making grants to these Societies, which in that year totalled £20,000 but which by 1859 had risen to £800,000. It was at this time that the curate at South Stoke, Reverend J. Trollope (1831-1844) put forward to Christ Church College proposals for a new schoolhouse and room. He had taken a census of the child population under 12 years old (because it was seldom found that a child remained at school after that age as they were required to work on the land) and found 110 children. Only 10 could be educated through the Higgs' charity. It only produced £18 per annum in the late 1830s. Reverend Trollope's idea was to provide education to the 10 and then as many as wished could also attend for a reasonable charge thus providing enough remuneration for a school master to devote himself entirely to the school. He estimated a total of 50 children.

In May of 1840 the curate was able to notify the College that The National Society had decided to help build the school providing £40 towards the schoolroom alone. Christ Church eventually provided £90 in two tranches towards the builder's estimate (for the school building and cottage) of £145.6.6d. Surprisingly, Isaac King was to give up some of his land, for this building work, for a small rent. By September of the same year the schoolroom was finished. It was of brick, 24ft x15ft and had a privy, coal store and boundary fence. The costing included provision of desks and fittings; and the school was located on what is now the playground of the present school. The first schoolmaster recorded in the school logbook in 1843 was Elisha Stevens, followed by David Lewis about 1845-1847 and by 1852 by James Fullbrook who taught 51 pupils.[3]

In January of 1852 another of South Stoke's curates, the Reverend George Fell noted that the weekly and Sunday school have endowments of 19 acres valued at £16.8.0d per annum which *"was not enough to fund a schoolmaster who should receive not less than £40 per annum"*. He noted that the local farmers were not well off financially and could not help, apart from Isaac King. He, however, was opposed to the Church of England and devoted all his efforts to a *"Dissenters' school"* in the next parish. This was the British School built in 1850 to accommodate 100 boys and girls in the centre of Goring with a brick and flint cottage next door for the teacher. The site and building works cost £306 and Jane Burgess was its first mistress. A teacher who would have been a *"judicious Christian woman of Dissenting Principles who has been trained for her work"*.[4] There is still a plaque over what is now a shop stating *"Goring and South Stoke British School supported by Voluntary Contributions Erected 1850"*. Isaac King encouraged his own labourers to send their children to that school.

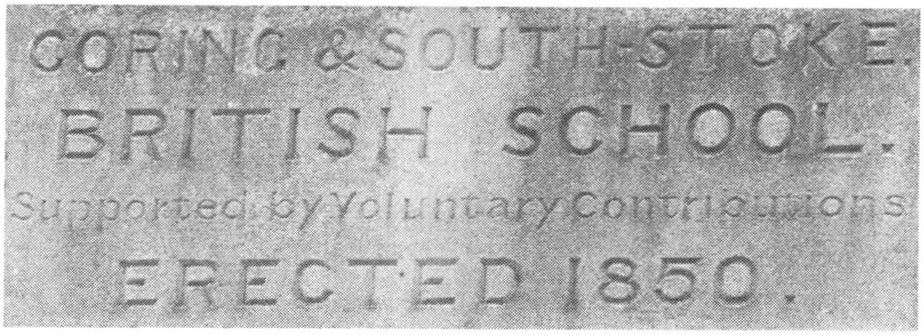

James Howes the minister for the Goring Free Church as well as the South Stoke Chapel wrote explaining why a school was needed- *"For many years past great power has been exercised by the clergy over the children of the poor whose parents attend chapel with us and so far was this carried that our members were never allowed to take their children with them to chapel at any time whatever. If a child was known to attend chapel, it was reprimanded for the first offence and turned out of their school for the second"*.[5] This explanation probably rang true for both parishes.

The British School now a shop showing plaque above entrance

In the Christ Church Estate Diaries of 1858 the curate, who is now Reverend Stafford Hilliard, made representations to the College for help in funding the South Stoke school. He stated the school mistress, Elizabeth Hewett was paid for by the vicar, Rev. Nind (though still not living in the village) but the whole cost of maintaining the school fell upon the poor curate. Again the name of the Dissenter, Isaac King was brought up him being a College tenant who did *"all he could to frustrate the church"*. The vicar himself, rather than the numerous curates, now seems to take an interest in the village's education, for at the start of 1860 plans were afoot to build a new replacement school. This was to be located where the current South Stoke Primary School building is situated, (2020). The local builder, Moses Winter of Wallingford, stated the schoolroom would be large enough for 60 children, he being of the view that in an agricultural community of 360, that would be all that would be allowed to attend. Furthermore, these scholars would be very young as poor parents needed to send their children out to work at the *"earliest period"*.

On 1st July 1862 Rev. Nind notified Christ Church that the new school built on their land was nearly complete and they provided £270, in the coming months, towards the building works which cost over £500. The National Society gave £25. Unlike the Dissenting British School in Goring where voluntary subscriptions paid for all the building works, in South Stoke they were thin on the ground. The vicar noted that there had only been two subscribers – Mr. Spearink and Mr. Spokes. (If it is known that they were the churchwardens make of this what you will). These gentlemen and the vicar were to be the trustees of the new school. The schoolmistress was to receive £30 per annum (provided by *"the children's pence"*) and a furnished house. This was Elizabeth Hewitt who moved from teaching in the old 1840 school building to the new. Subscriptions amounted to £5.10.0d plus a government grant of £8.13.1d and any deficit was met by the incumbent vicar.

Image of the 1862 school taken before 1881

In 1862 the schools' grant system became linked to academic results based on exams - *"Payment by Results"*. The school received so much money dependent on the children's success. Attendance was also linked to how much grant was provided. The Log and Board Minute Books of the early 20th century attest to the preoccupation with these exams and the children's attendance. William Forster's Education Act of 1870, whilst leaving all existing schools intact and even increasing their grants, now set up an entirely new school system that of State or Board schools - to be built, financed and run by local elected boards, with funds from local rates. It was at this time that Miss M.J. Franklin was South Stoke's headteacher. In 1867 she had 53 pupils -28 boys and 25 girls paying a penny a week towards their schooling. Primary education was now to become established on a national level, with the new network of State schools supplementing the existing voluntary Church schools. South Stoke kept its Church of England National School until 1877 even though in 1875 the Council on Education ordered the compulsory formation of a School Board in the parish.[6] The Dissenters' British School fell by the wayside with the government legislation. The 1870 Act required the British School to employ a certificated teacher and despite advertising as late as 1878 for such a mistress[7] the person did not materialise. Failure to comply meant the Education Department would cause a School Board to be formed for the Goring School District (1874). The school managed to continue until 1884 but by then the pupil numbers were in decline and times were changing.

In 1880 school attendance was at last made compulsory for all children between the ages of 5 and 10 but even twenty years later, South Stoke parents were being summonsed for not sending their children to school. Nevertheless, by 1886 there were throughout the country some four and a half million children attending school compared with one and a half million in 1870 - progress indeed! School fees were still required however and it was not until 1900 that education became free.

In 1887 Mrs. Margaretta Griffiths was recorded as the head teacher of the school with its 55 pupils.[8] She was still listed in the county directories of 1891 but by 1894 Charles Henry Humpage had taken over the headship.[9] He was assisted by his wife Lucy and a Miss Florence Page who was at the school for at least the whole of 1898 but resigned as assistant mistress in the June of 1899.[10] Towards the end of the nineteenth century school numbers had risen to 80 children plus and the HMI Reports regularly use phrases such as *"The main room is full to overflowing and will probably have to be enlarged"*.

School pre-1906; the ivy clad wing was the Master's house

Converting the master's home into classroom facilities does not appear to have occurred until 1906. Meantime, the stern disciplinarian, Mr Fred Charles Sommerton together with his wife-to-be Jessie Russell took on the headship in August of 1899 at a joint salary of £120 p.a.. In that Autumn Term William Costiff wrote twice to the School Board to try to obtain a job for his daughter at the school. Eventually he was successful; Miss Kate Costiff commenced her employment as an 18 year old (she is thought to be standing second from the right on the back row of the photo overleaf). She taught the infants. Kate never married but lived with her parents at Dilkhush Cottage next door to the school. She devoted most of her working life to teaching serving under all subsequent head teachers up to and including Florence Naish who worked into the 1960s. Kate, herself, finally retired at the age of 72 in 1953. However, in 1918, Kate did resign in order *"to take up a new sphere of work in London"*. She only returned to her old job at the beginning of 1925 much to the relief of the then head Mr Kilby. She was remembered with great affection by all who passed through the school during her time there. Her house became popularly known as Kate's Cottage and still bears that name to-day.

Class photo pre-1906, showing the Master's house in close up

After Mr Sommerton's resignation there was an era between 1903 and the April of 1906 when another couple came and went -Mr and Mrs Ernest Crook.

On a national basis reforms to secondary education occurred in 1902 with Balfour's Education Act, when a countrywide system was set up, as had previously occurred with primary education. At the same time the local School Boards were abolished and both primary and secondary education were placed under Local Authority control. However, the land and school buildings remained the property of St. Andrew's Church in South Stoke; and from 1906 (when the rent was fixed at 10/- p.a.) to the present day the County Council has been paying an appropriate and ever increasing rent to the Church.

In South Stoke there now followed a period of some stability with the school personnel (though with the resignation of Miss Costiff until her return the infant teaching left much to be desired and this impacted on the progress of the juniors). From 1906 until his retirement in 1927 Lawrence Thomas Kilby was appointed head, assisted by his wife Madeline.

Post-1906 building works but pre-1920, the playground is now divided

The master's school house was now no longer available for use and although the Kilbys found accommodation in Woodcote initially, the School Managers thought that it was too far away. Mr Bullock offered to rent his newly built house to them in the village (now known as Turret House but originally called The Rise) which they accepted.

Turret House, formerly The Rise, is situated at the south end of the village

The school was organised into three classes the Infants, the Lower and the Upper classes. Subjects taught and examined termly were English consisting of Reading, Recitation, Grammar and Composition, Arithmetic, History, Geography, Nature Subjects, Drawing, Plasticine Modelling and Physical Training. The older boys were taught gardening from 1906 and after an HMI Report in 1926 woodworking lessons commenced, again for the boys only. The girls did needlework.

Donald Paradise followed on from Mr Kilby in April of 1927 but only stayed until the end of the Summer Term 1928. Mr Fred Parsons originally took up his post as a temporary head but by November this was made a permanent appointment. However, in a matter of months the school was to lose this Head. After the Easter holidays on 8th April 1929 South Stoke became a *"Junior"* School taking children only up to the age of 11years old. Mr Parsons was to take charge of *"South Stoke Woodcote Council School"* and with him went 16 senior children who were being transferred to that school.

It was not until Butler's Education Act of 1944 that secondary education became automatic for all children from the ages of 11 to 15. In the early decades of the twentieth century pupils at South Stoke School had normally left as soon as they reached the age of 14 to start work, the boys to the farms and the girls going into service or helping at home. Even in the 1830s Rev. Trollope was stating that parents would take their children out of school in order to join the workforce and so provide money for the family. This was echoed in the 1850s at the British School claiming the boys' attendance was *"greatly interfered with at the busy seasons of the year"*. More than half a century later and Mr Kilby bemoans the same situation. What is known today as the summer holidays was called the harvest holidays in the early decades of the 20th century. It was a 5 week break at the end of July and it literally was in order to bring in the harvest. However the school log book shows that this can be a moveable feast. 9th July 1915 *"a few of the boys have been absent to assist the farmers in the hayfield"*. The harvest holiday commences 30th July and yet a log entry for 10th September states *"for the last three days nine boys have been working in the fields and the greater part of them are under 12 years of age".* In 1916 the disruption to the school day was even earlier-haymaking was ongoing by 22nd June with boys absent until early October.

Throughout the Great War years the boys were regularly helping the local farmers but this was never alluded to by the headmaster. For him, it was exasperating complaining to the vicar and the attendance officer. By 1919-1920 Mr Kilby stated this absenteeism was illegal and the attendance officer had to deal with the farmers as well as the parents. However from the 1920s on there is little mention of this problem re-occurring.

Miss Florence M. Stanbury took over the village school in 1929 as a young 25 year old head but with Kate Costiff by her side she need not have worried. The HMI reports are positively glowing for the work achieved at the school. Miss Stanbury eventually became Mrs Naish and was to remain head until 1967.

Between 1913 (according to the school log book) and 1920 school numbers were in the 70s-80s. By the 1920s the numbers were in the 50s-60s. After 1929 the pupils over 11 years of age went to Woodcote for their education which meant the 1930s would produce smaller numbers on roll (30s-40s). By 1970 the number of pupils was averaging around 50 and there was a staff of three qualified teachers. But since then, numbers have fluctuated between the upper 50s and lower 20s. Indeed by 1985 numbers at the school had fallen to such a low level with 22, that there was once again a real threat of closure by the Local Education Authority believing the resultant saving of funds could be better utilised elsewhere, with South Stoke children being taken by bus to neighbouring schools. Originally the threats of closure were regarding the difficulties over the emptying of the lavatory buckets in the outside toilets. This was a problem according to the log book causing worries throughout the 20th century. This was a public health hazard. It was not until 1967 that the situation was finally resolved with modern sanitation being installed within the school building.

By 1986 pupil numbers had risen to 28 and this, together with a vigorous campaign mounted by the school governors, led to closure being averted. Since the latter half of the 20th century and into the 21st the school has been run (with the assistance of helpers) by Peter Long 1967-69, assisted by Miss Cunningham, Miss Betty Tidbury acting head during 1969, Christopher Romney 1970-78 assisted by Mrs Mowforth and Mrs Saunders, Mr Machin during 1978, Paul Overton 1979-1983, Peter Smith 1984-87, Mr Machin again for one term, followed by Mrs Jackie Friend from April 1988 until her retirement.

The current head, Miss Amanda Rogers took over in 2004. School numbers are fairly constant around 40 but gone are the days when the establishment was full of village children. The fluctuation of school numbers over the past forty years was *"due in the main to the difficulties of local, young married couples obtaining suitable accommodation within the village"*. It is still a truism today coupled now with the introduction of parental choice and competition between schools due to the introduction of the Local Management of Schools with the Education Reform Act of 1988. Continuity in the village still exists in that today's education still takes place in the 1860s building though now fully modernised inside and out. It is still positioned next to the Church and in its prominent position on the main street.

ENDNOTES:

1. Victoria County History.

2. Appendix to The 1st Report of The Commissioners on The Education of The Poor Dec.1818 (accessed on line).

3. By 1853 Lascelles' Oxford Directory records Mr Fullbrook as having an average of 80 scholars in his charge.

4. Certainly this was the requirement in an advert used 10 years later for her replacement - Reading Mercury 14th July 1860.

5. James Howes to the Editor *of "Religious Intelligence"* 5th June 1850.

6. 15th May 1875 Reading Mercury, Oxford Gazette.

7. 22nd June 1878 Advert for British School in the Reading Mercury.

8. Kelly's Directory of Berks., Bucks. And Oxon.1887.

9. The Oxfordshire Evening News 26th December 1894. Mr Humpage was the returning officer for the parish council elections held in The School Room.

10. S254/1/A1/1 The School Board Minute Book Feb.1898-Dec.1902, at the Oxfordshire Heritage Centre.

For further reading see Appendix 2, Reminiscences: South stoke school 1890 to 1987.

APPENDIX 1

THE EYNSHAM CARTULARY: REFERENCES TO SOUTH STOKE

A cartulary or chartulary (Latin: cartularium or chartularium), is a medieval manuscript, volume or roll (rotulus) containing transcriptions of original documents relating to the foundation, privileges, and legal rights of ecclesiastical establishments, municipal corporations, industrial associations, institutions of learning, or families. The term is sometimes also applied to collections of original documents bound in one volume or attached to one another so as to form a roll, as well as to custodians of such collections.[1]

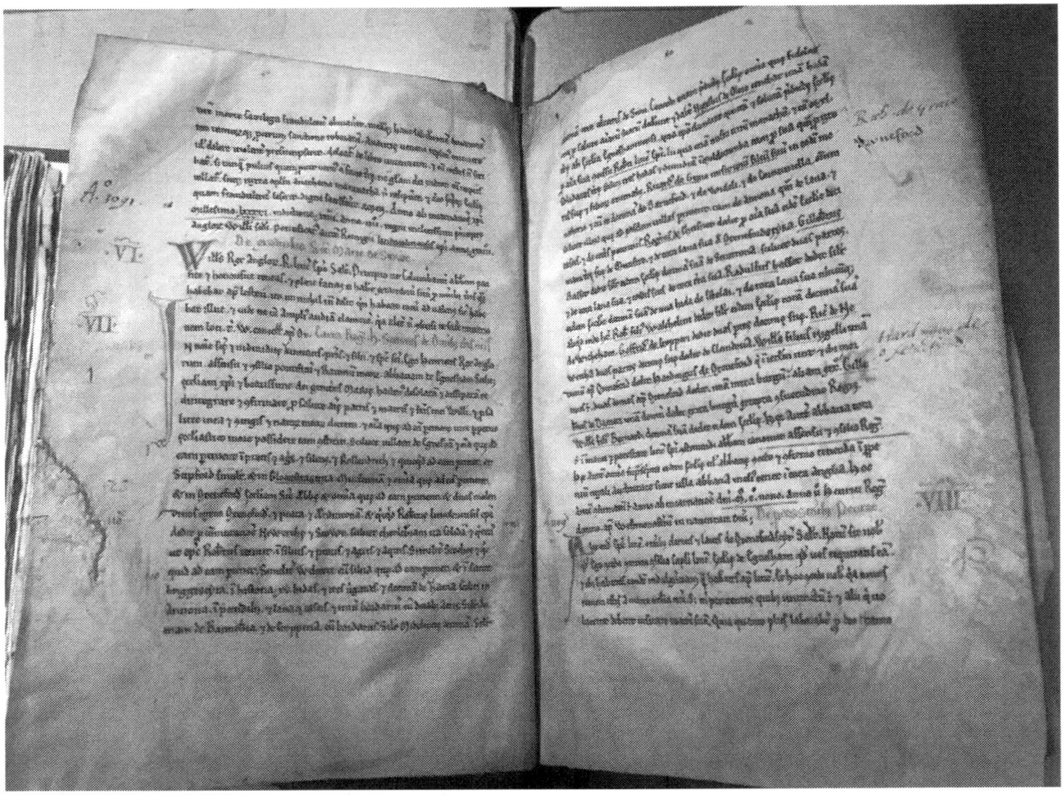

The original Cartulary of Eynsham Abbey (image opposite) was in two parchment volumes, written in Latin, which provided information on the history of the Abbey and its possessions since it was founded in 1005. Both these cartularies are still preserved in the library of the Dean and Chapter of Christ Church, Oxford; covering a period from the 12th to the early 16th centuries, and providing valuable records of the Abbey up to its dissolution in 1538.

In 1907 the Rev. H E Salter MA produced in two volumes an edited copy of the Eynsham Cartulary, again written in Latin and printed for the Oxford Historical Society by the Clarendon Press. Salter described the contents of the first cartulary as *"begun before the end of the 12th century, deeds were added to it continually as they were given or received"*: and said that the second cartulary contained information *"about the manors farmed by the Abbey in about 1360, the size and condition of the lands and fields, the nature and value of the services of the villein and the estimated profits; all described in detail"*.

Mrs Pat A Dando of the previous South Stoke Historical Society collated from Salter's two volumes all relevant references to South Stoke, with help from Simon J J Corcoran, who translated the Latin text. The first reference of interest in Salter is that, following Eynsham's acquisition of Stoke in 1094 from Bishop Bloet of Lincoln, mention is made that in 1189 Bishop Hugh of Lincoln was confirmed as holding all the churches in Oxfordshire; including *"the churches which are situated in the demesne villages of the Abbey of Eynsham, namely the church of Eynsham with its chapels, the church of Stoke and the church of Charlbury"*.

Accordingly, from 1186 to 1227 Eynsham (as deputy of the bishop) was to appoint its first three vicars to Stoke, namely Ralph, Osbert and Walter. Thereafter the village was known as Bishopstoke, and an entry of 1213 referred to it as such.

The earliest reference to Stoke in the cartulary is an entry of 1109 which, in a *"Charter of King Henry the Elder concerning all our lands"*, confirms that *"whatever Robert Bishop of Lincoln gave in exchange for Norwich and Stowe, namely Charlbury ... in woods and meadows and fields and waters, similarly at Stoke and whatever pertains to it"* shall belong to Eynsham. Further entries of 1189 and 1197 merely confirm that Bishop Hugh of Lincoln was responsible for *"the church of Stoke"* and for *"the pension in it of 1 pound of pepper"*; also that the church was *"free from all Episcopal imposts and only pays 8 shillings for Peter's pence"*. Between 1213 and 1227 there are detailed descriptions of land made over to the Abbey by Thomas Frankelanus of Bishopstoke. The names of several of the roads and lands mentioned in these deeds exist to this day; and some of the deeds in question are respectively witnessed by Ralph and later Osbert, *"parsons of Stoke"*. There is also a first mention in 1220 of *"the mill next to the land of Stephen de la Mare"*.

In 1264 the Abbey made over to William de la Barre *"the whole of the messuage in the village of Stoke ... with the adjacent croft and park, containing two acres, and with all its other appurtenances"*. The de la Barre family were thereafter to live in Barre Place (later the Manor House), and gave their name to the adjoining road and Barre pond. By now the village was a rectory in the Abbey's patronage, and from 1251 onwards rectors were appointed and the village became known as Stoke Abbas. It was subsequently called South Stoke so as to distinguish it from North Stoke and Little Stoke. In an entry of 1264, in which John le Justice *"demised and quit-claim"* of all his lands to the Abbey, the village is first referred to as Stoke Abbas. In 1252 there is mention of *"village, fields and woodland of Stoke and Woodcote"*. This refers to the fact that, from earliest times, Woodcote was always a part of Stoke parish. In 1270 details of tithes belonging to Eynsham are set out, with names of various fields and landowners in Stoke Abbas. In 1279 a cartulary entry records that *"the Abbot of Eynsham holds the whole village of Stoke, with 2 hides of arable land and with 9 acres of meadow and half the Thames in demesne, namely from the mill of Stoke Marmyon up to Mereway; also he holds 50 acres of woodland and 60 acres of heath in common. (A reference to Woodcote). Also he holds one windmill"*.

The same entry of 1279 states that the Abbot *"held all the above-named in exchange (for Stow) from the Bishop of Lincoln; and he holds all the aforesaid from the aforesaid bishop in fee. And the said Abbot makes suit in the Hundred of Dorchester every three weeks"*. By 1321 the village is referred to as South Stoke Abbas, with the change of name clearly under way. An entry of 1366 confirms that *"the Abbot and convent of Eynsham hold the manor of Stoke in pure and perpetual almoign[2] in chief from the Lord Bishop of Lincoln; for which manor the Abbot is held to suit of the Hundred of Dorchester"*. This entry continues to record that *"the said Lord Abbot and convent are patrons of the church there and have the right of presentation to the church whenever it is vacant; and that the same Abbot and convent take half of all the sheaf tithes of the whole parish"*. It also mentions; *"that the rector holds there the manse with its enclosure, and it contains four acres and two virgates of land with appurtenances joined to his rectory"*. Indeed from 1251 to 1390 some nine rectors of the parish were appointed by the Abbot.

This 1366 entry continues with comprehensive details of tithes payable in Stoke; and then goes on to refer to the manor, which *"consists of the following rights, appurtenances and portions; namely that the said manor is sufficiently built, as to hall, chambers, kitchen, grange and other outhouses for various functions; and contains 2 acres less 12 perches and a half, and is valued annually at 6 shillings and 8 pence; and they say that there are three fields there, namely the southern field, the middle field and the northern field; of which two are sown annually, while the third lies fallow".* There then follow long and detailed descriptions of the land in each of the three open fields, with acreages and values of each named furlong (a group of strips). Details follow of the meadow the lord *has "above the Thames"*, and of the four acres of pastureland he holds. There is mention that the *"lord has fishing rights, namely half of the Thames from Le Meredicche, between the bounds of Little Stoke and the edge of the Manor of Stoke Abbas, and continues as far as Romisford ... plus one small island at the edge of the lord's meadow called Coveyt".* There is a note of the *"woodland at Exlade"* which the lord also has; and finally of *"one windmill in disrepair, at which all villein tenants of Stoke and Woodcote are obliged to grind".* There then follows a most comprehensive list of some 54 tenants of the manor and of the rents they paid, all these details of land and tenants running to some 18 pages.

Other earlier records of 1152, 1311, 1320, 1321 and 1333 all record various transfers of land between individuals, and to or from the Abbey. In 1239 it is stated that the Abbey received from the church of Stoke a pension of one pound of pepper and a portion of the lesser tithes. In 1256 *"the profits of the demesne land in stoke totalled £4-15".* In 1269 Eynsham received a total annual income from Stoke of £31-19-2, including that from *"a woodland and one mill".*

In 1399 Bishop Beaufort, patron of the Abbey, authorised Eynsham to institute a vicarage at Stoke, where the vicar *"shall officiate the cure of souls of the parish church of Stoke Abbas"* and *"shall take and have all and every manner of tithes both greater and lesser"*. Also he *"shall have from the glebe and endowed demesne lands pertaining to the said church 8 acres of arable land fully without deduction of tithes"*. This land is then described in detail. The deed goes on to say that the vicar *"will provide and maintain one lamp burning in the chancel of the said church, and bread and wine ... for the celebration of divine service and the communion of the parishioners"*. In addition the vicar is assigned *"a manse adequate for the housing of himself and his own"*, in which the existing rector was living, *"namely the hall and chambers existing in the northern part and the garden limited by bounds and margins"*.

The church at South Stoke was now in the Abbey's possession, where it remained until the Abbey was dissolved in 1539. During this time some 16 vicars were appointed. In 1530 it was said that the rent from Stoke's demesne land was £5-13-4, whilst the tithes of the rectory amounted to £10-10. In 1536 Eynsham granted the lease of church and manor for 80 years to Walter Barton (earlier such leases had been granted in 1460 and 1476). After the Abbey's dissolution its lands were given to Christ Church, which continued the practice of leasing out the manor. Today the Victoria County History has a lengthy entry on South Stoke and has clearly used much of the information in Salter's Eynsham Cartulary, which it has elaborated upon and explained in detail.

ENDNOTES:

1. The Oxford English Dictionary definition

2. Almoign meaning: tenure of land held in perpetuity by the Abbot in return for prayers for the donors' soul and his descendants.

APPENDIX 2

REMINISCENCES: SOUTH STOKE SCHOOL 1890-1987

Introduction

Reminiscences of the school by people living in the village have been provided over the years. In the early 1960s members of the Over 60s Club in South Stoke (the Happy Circle) put into writing their memories of life in South Stoke over the period from around 1890 to 1914. Understandably these memories included many recollections of the village school, which was the daily pivot of the children's lives. In the late 1980s a South Stoke Historical Society was set up to research the history of South Stoke. As part of this research local villagers provided their recollection of their lives in South Stoke and these reminiscences are also included here to cover the period into the 1970s. The presentation is completed with the reminiscences of the two head teachers in post from 1979 to 1987. Oral interviews relating to later periods were undertaken by the South Stoke Historical Society of the late 1980s and now by the Society that was resurrected in 2015.

Reminiscences of the Happy Circle (1890-1914 plus)

The source of these comments is the information provided by the members of the Happy Circle, but all comments are not sourced to the individual members. Comments used in quotes are taken from the actual source documents. *"In the early days the schoolmaster lived in part of the building and there was only one schoolroom for the children's use;*

so, in the 1890s the Village Hall was used for some classes. A few years later the school was enlarged and a separate house provided for the master. In about 1907 there were 90 pupils, the number rising to 99 at the time of the 1st World War. At that time Mr. Kilby was the Master and taught the boys, with his wife being in charge of the senior girls; whilst two assistants the Misses Costiff looked after the juniors and infants. Sometimes children started school at the age of 3; whilst the leaving age varied, being dependent on when they had to start work, some boys leaving at 10 to work on a farm and girls leaving at 13 to go into service".

As was normal at that time the curriculum basically covered the three Rs, reading, 'riting, 'rithmetic. However, as one member of the Happy Circle has recalled: "*It included, in addition to the normal subjects, gardening for the senior boys and sewing for the girls; the latter were also taught the theory of cooking, but this was not a popular subject as they would much rather have done some practical work. A school Prize Giving was held annually, at which a bronze medal was given to each pupil who had never missed a day's work, or even been late for school. Any child who earned such a medal for five consecutive years would get a silver watch*". Frank Geall received such a watch as did May Maskell at a slightly later date of 1914, for 10 years perfect attendance.

The attendance medal of Dorothea Allum for four consecutive years, on the right.

The fact that it was considered quite normal for children to earn these awards seems to testify to the good health and behaviour of pupils in those days.

The boy in this early school photo appears to be wearing attendance medals

One child who was late getting to school in 1947 described how she was held up by the great flood of that year, and only finally got there by going through Manor Farm and the churchyard to reach the back of the school.

The Street flooded in 1947, the school was on the left

As well as their schoolwork, the children had plenty of organised sports and their own games as well; "*more so it seems and more fun than the children get today. In the early years of the century there was a girls' cricket team, made up of senior girls and captained by Miss Nind, the Vicar's daughter, which played a number of matches against other villages. A regular summer event was the school Sports Day, which was held in the Park (the field belonging to Manor Farm adjacent to the Village Hall). After this, tea would always be provided at the Farm by Mr. and Mrs. George Bullock and Mr. and Mrs. Wilson. The usual games that were played included skipping, marbles, spinning tops, hopscotch, bowling hoops, tip and run, baseball and pole the cat*". A Swimming Club was also organised in the 1930s by Mrs. Naish to encourage the children to learn to swim. The children also used to take part in plays organised by the village's Dramatic Society.

Singing games included Oranges and Lemons, In and Out of the Window and The Old Soldier from Botany Bay. On their way to school or after lessons there were many exciting things for the children to do: "*There was boat building to watch by the river, the smithy to loiter by under two big chestnut trees in the Street, and the carpenter/undertaker to gaze at while he went about his business of making coffins. Along the bridlepath could be found Nebuchadnezzar the donkey, pumping up water for Mr. Cook at Willow Grange (now Bridleway House); whilst down by the river could be seen the horses (for towing barges) being brought over on the ferry from Moulsford*". The children also loved watching the great trains of the GWR thundering through the village; whilst the footpath that led under the railway, through the tunnel known as the "*bogey hole*", was a cause of excitement to some and fear to others.

Sunday was of course a busy day, since *"all the children in the village went to Sunday School at the Church, usually staying on for Morning Service. Then in the afternoon they would often go to Sunday school at the Chapel. At one time Mr. and Mrs. Brock (a farming family living at the Elms - long since demolished and replaced by modern bungalows) held a regular Sunday school in the Village Hall; and used to give those attending a Christmas treat, complete with tree and presents for those with highest marks"*. *Then there were the other holidays and high days which the children loved: "Shrove Tuesday, when they would go round collecting pennies and singing Knick Knack the Pans hot ..., May Day, which was always celebrated at the school; the Chapel Sunday School outing, when the children would be taken in farm wagons to nearby places of interest for a picnic; and Guy Fawkes Day, when a bonfire high as a house would be lit on the Recreation Ground and fireworks/refreshments would be provided"*. Lastly there would be Christmas with its family festivities.

Pre-1906 May Day celebrations

As regards May Day, the senior class at the school used to select various names, which were then put to the vote of the whole school. *"The girl with the largest number of votes was elected Queen, and her unsuccessful rivals became her attendants (these varied from two to six). On the day the May Queen set out from home in a donkey cart decorated with flowers. Her bodyguard comprised two boys, dressed in their best and carrying imitation swords of gold, silver and blue. Behind them came the Maids of Honour and then a little child carrying the Queen's crown. Then followed all the other children, the girls in white frocks, socks and shoes, with wreaths of flowers in their hair. At the school playground, where the Maypole was erected, the crowning ceremony then took place, followed by dancing round the maypole by chosen children, whilst the others sang May Day songs. Afterwards there was a procession round the village, a tea party and then sports"*.

Reminiscences collected by the South Stoke Historical Society (1988-1991)

The Society undertook an oral history project and the results are detailed below. Maiden names are shown in brackets.

Jessie (Vickery) Dawe from 1909:

Other South Stoke residents have taken the trouble to write up notes of their recollections of school days in the village. One of the earliest is from Mrs. Jessie Dawe (nee Vickery). She was one of the large Vickery family who was to marry Aubrey Dawe, who had been trading as butcher in the village since the 1920s.

The Vickery's home opposite the school now known as Devonshire House

Together they took over Mossons, the local grocery and post office, which they were to run for nearly 30 years before retiring. Jessie started school in 1909 when she was five and was to stay there until fourteen. She well remembers Lawrence Kilby and his wife and three children, who all lived at The Rise, rented from George Bullock of Manor Farm. The Kilbys taught the older children, whilst Kate Costiff taught the infants. Lawrence Kilby had the seniors in the main room, divided into 3 classes, whilst Madeline Kilby took the juniors in the adjacent room. Kate taught the infants in a separate room, once occupied by Mr. Humpage and his family. There were nearly 90 pupils at the school then.

Jessie recalls that "*the Kilbys were dedicated, strict teachers, who kept the children well under control. They were made to work hard but were very happy there. School started every day at 9am with the singing of a hymn, and there would be a 10-minute break in mid-morning. Lessons would end at*

1pm when Grace would be said, before the children went home for dinner, returning at 1.45, and School would end at 3.45pm. During the break and dinner hour, games were played on the playground, but in those days, there were no swimming lessons. On one afternoon a week Mrs. Kilby took the girls for sewing lessons, which took place in the infants' classroom". Jessie well remembers the May Day celebrations when the May Queen was selected and all the children walked up to Willow Grange, singing songs as they went, to collect the donkey and cart: then back to the school for the Maypole Dance. "*We girls all had to dress up in white for the occasion, and the day itself could often be a very cold one. However, I was never chosen to be the Queen, and I don't think any of my sisters were ever chosen either*".

Post-1906 maypole dancing in the school playground

Throughout Jessie's time at school, the Kilbys were in charge. After that she was away at work and only came home at weekends, so she never really knew Mr. Parsons or Mr. Paradise. However, she remembers Florence Stanbury taking over in 1929, especially as she then came to live with the Vickery family in Devonshire House and recalls her getting married in 1935. By then Jessie was also married and living in South Stoke. "*My sister Joan and Florence were great friends and my daughter Christine went to Mrs. Naish's school in due course, where she stayed until she was 11. After Kate Costiff left the school another of my sisters, Laura, taught the infants for a while. (February 1920–31st December 1924). My niece, Betty Tidbury, also did a teaching spell there in 1969*". Jessie and all her friends were to hold Florence Naish in very high esteem.

Peggy (Margaret King) Peplar 1915-1925:

Another lady who lived in the village all her life and who was also at school with the Kilbys is Mrs. Peggy Peplar. Some of her fondest memories are of the infant teacher Kate Costiff. "*She was tall, thin, with very dark hair and never seemed to change. Indeed, she looked exactly the same when my own three children were to be taught by her many years later! I think she was a wonderful infant teacher*". Her earliest recollections of Mr. Kilby are when she was in Kate's class and would suddenly "*see a face with a pointed beard peering through the window between the infants room and the big room next door: it was Mr. Kilby, checking to see all was in order with us infants!*" In due course she moved from the infant's class to that "*big room next door, where I started at standard I and was to work my way to standard VII. As I progressed my ambition was always to arrive at those big, high windows facing south; a prestige position, which was always, regarded by us children as a terrific step up!*"

Post-1920, flagpole and divided playground

She remembers how, on arrival at the school in the morning, the children would line up by the flagpole, boys on the left and girls on the right (separated by a fence), before marching to school for Assembly when hymns would be sung. They had a break at 11 a.m. when they would go out onto the playground for games; and at midday they all went home for dinner. During the afternoon there would be another break before school finished at 4 p.m. In those days the Kilbys lived with their three children in The Rise, until the Bullock family needed it once more for Misses May and Eva, when they moved into the Corner House. Peggy too remembers the sewing classes that Mrs. Kilby used to run for the girls; and recalls on certain days the boys would go off to the school allotments (opposite to The Rise and where the house called Herons was later to be built). She also remembers the awards for good behaviour and regular attendance, and the frequent visits that the vicar, Hubert Nind, would make to the school.

As with other contributors the memory that is most clear in Peggy's mind is of May Day celebrations, when the maypole would be brought down from the loft, and the old pedal organ would be carried out from the school for the Head to provide music. "*On the great day, which was nearly always cold, the children all assembled at the school with their mayday garlands, the best of which earned their owners presents. Then the May Queen would be selected and proudly take her place in the decorated donkey cart for the procession round the village. We used to end up at the Vicarage, where we sang Mayday songs on the lawn, before returning to the school for dancing round the Maypole*". Also, on that day Peggy remembers an old man, whom the children called "*Deafy*", coming out from Wallingford with his barrel organ to add zest to the festivities.

A particular memory of Mrs. Peplar's concerns the strict discipline imposed by Mr. Kilby and "*of his dreaded split cane, with which punishment was well and truly carried out with no discrimination of sex-though never as bad as that inflicted by Mr. Squeers of Dotheboys Hall in Dickens' Nicholas Nickelby*". Sometimes reports of children misbehaving in the village would reach the ears of the local Bobby, who would then visit the school to question those concerned. This usually led to the guilty ones being called out to be dealt with, "*an occurrence that seemed to be quite a frequent one*". In addition to May Day, Peggy also remembers the celebrations that were usually held on Empire Day, and the occasional outings that took place; "*one being a cycle ride for those pupils who had bicycles, which took them as far as Engelfield Park beyond Pangbourne*".

Raymond and Queenie (Eleanor Smith) Allum from 1916:

A long-established family in South Stoke, whose forbears go back some 300 years, are the Allums. Of the few that still remain in the village, both Raymond and his sister-in-law Eleanor (known to all as Queenie) have submitted some recollections of their schooldays. Queenie had five years at school from 1920, (according to the School Register she actually started school in 1916 and left in 1925). During that time she remembers Mr. Kilby as a stern disciplinarian. She recalls in particular the Church's influence on the school, her confirmation and happy times spent singing in the choir.

Ray, who returned home from German captivity as a POW in 1945 and who ran the old village shop (since demolished with Pillar Box House now on its site), assisted by Queenie, was also at school in the latter years of the Kilby era. His memories are much the same as Queenie's and he recalls Sunday School days and his interest in bellringing. He has two special memoirs of school life. "*One Saturday morning I was with George Vince in the village when he said he would like to go to the school to see his mother, who used to clean there on Saturdays. So, I went there with him, and after a while he said "look, here are next week's sums which I have found". So, we took note of them, and as they were put to our class during the following week, we got them all right! But after that, without such help, we got them all wrong and that usually meant the cane! Then I remember a freezing day in winter when we tipped over the water butt that stood at the corner of the school. As the water ran down over the playground it froze and made a grand slide*".

Eric Small in the 1920s:

Further reminiscences were collected by the previous South Stoke Historical Society from those in the village with memories of their schooldays. One such was Eric Small; whose grandfather came to work on a farm at South Stoke at the turn of the 20th century. Eric's father worked at Lower Farm and lived at Waises Cottage, where Eric was born in 1920. As an under four-year-old he started school in Mr. Kilby's time and can remember Mr. and Mrs. Kilby being presented with a table at a special ceremony on their retirement in 1927. "*They were much liked*" he says, although Mr. Kilby was a rare man for discipline. He was followed by Mr. Paradise and Mr. Parsons. The latter was rather odd as he insisted on caning troublesome pupils in their own homes! He was replaced in 1929 by the legendary Miss Stanbury. She was especially interested in sports and keep fit activities, which were now encouraged as never before to the delight of the children. As mentioned earlier she was also instrumental in setting up the local Swimming Club, with appropriate facilities, on the bank of the Thames below the Vicarage. "*Here a diving board and a tower were put up, also a boom within which children could learn to swim in safety. Here they were taught to swim by being suspended in the water, strapped into a suitable*

harness, from a pole held by the instructor. Lifebelts were provided, also a portable changing room that could be taken away in the winter. This was a popular activity, but came to an end in the late 1950s when swimming pools became available in the vicinity – at Carmel College and Turner's Court. Sports and games in general took place on Friday afternoons at the "school meadow" behind Devonshire House, with the permission of William Bullock whose land it was". Eric Small also remembers Empire Day, 24th May, being always celebrated with special events; and Mrs. Naish's interest in teaching geography and weather patterns. "*She was also very keen on all aspects of country life, and taught us about the birds, plants, animals and insects*".

Nancy (Fox) Hunt from 1926:

Another local lady who had spent all her life in the village is Nancy Hunt (nee Fox). She attended school from 1926 under a succession of teachers from Lawrence Kilby to Florence Stanbury. Like so many others her clearest memory is of Kate Costiff and her infant class, "*which had its own room, heated in winter by a large stove. When the weather was especially cold Kate's mother would bring cups of hot cocoa for the children from her cottage next door; she would also make Christmas puddings for the infants at Christmas time. In those days Florence taught the juniors; and many years later I got to know her (Mrs. Naish as she was by then) quite well, as she was in charge of the school when my own daughters went there*". Nancy especially remembers Empire Day at school, when all the children would all walk past the Union Jack, flying from the flagpole in the playground, to salute it. Also, on that day, she says, "*we all wore little miniature flags pinned to our dresses*". When her own children were at school Nancy took an especial interest in the administration side of school affairs and became a Governor.

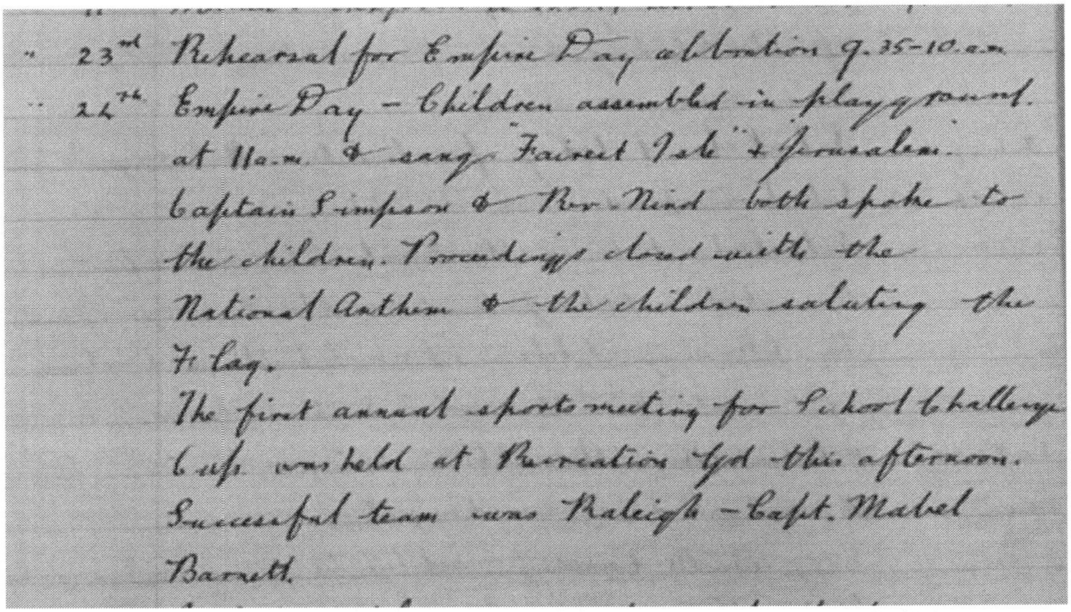
" 23rd Rehearsal for Empire Day celebration 9.35-10.a.m.
" 24th Empire Day - Children assembled in playground at 11a.m. & sang "Fairest Isle" & Jerusalem. Captain Simpson & Rev. Reid both spoke to the children. Proceedings closed with the National Anthem & the children saluting the Flag.
The first annual sports meeting for School Challenge Cup was held at Recreation Gd this afternoon. Successful team was Raleigh - Capt. Mabel Barnett.

School log book for Empire Day celebrations in May c.1927/28

This says Nancy, "*was during the years 1957-70, when we were pressing for improvements to the school buildings in general, and in particular for the provision of flush toilets*". She recalls that this latter problem especially dominated the efforts of the school governors for most of her period in office; "*with success finally being achieved in 1967, when a new toilet block and kitchen was finally constructed*". Two other notable events, which Nancy well remembers, "*were the award of the Dolphin Trophy for swimming to the school in 1966 and the retirement of Mrs. Naish at Easter, 1967*".

Iris (Peplar) Calder from 1926:

A contemporary at school with Nancy was Iris Calder (nee Peplar). Her mother and her two elder brothers had all been to the local school; but Iris admits she didn't greatly enjoy her own schooldays there from 1926-31, and as a result doesn't have many memories.

She of course remembers the Kilbys and Florence Stanbury, who on first arrival used to lodge with the Vickery family at Devonshire House. "*She married Mr. Naish, who was a sailor in the Merchant Navy: I liked him*", she says. She also, like so many others, well remembers Kate Costiff and her infant class, which was held "*in a separate and comfortable room, with a big black range*". She too recalls morning Assemblies and the May Day and Empire Day events. She was at school when swimming classes first began, but never really enjoyed them. Amongst her fellow pupils she especially remembers Richard and Joe Dunne, Eric Small, Laura Cox and Phyllis Swain.

Mrs. Florence (Stanbury) Naish 1929 to 1967:

There has already been much reference to Mrs. Naish, the much loved and longest serving of all South Stoke's head teachers. In February of 1989, she gave a very clear and lucid interview, in which she described in considerable detail her work for the children of South Stoke. It is only appropriate that her reminiscences, which are so full of interest, should be repeated here at some length. Florence was born in Exeter in 1906, and then moved with her parents to Wallingford, where she was educated at the Grammar School. From there she took up a teaching post at the Benson school as an uncertified teacher and was to study by post for a teaching qualification. The subjects she took were principles of teaching, needlework, geography, music, maths, history and science. She did well in her exams, with distinction in the two latter subjects, and then applied in 1929 for the vacant post of head teacher at South Stoke.

To her amazement she was accepted for the post, though she felt very inexperienced on arrival in comparison with Kate Costiff, who had already taught there for so many years with such skill and knowledge. Florence was to find her a great help and was always to consult with her and seek her advice. They were to become life-long friends, with each respecting the other's judgement. Florence lodged with the Vickery family in Devonshire House (across the road from the school), and was to find her new pupils to be "*country children with few manners*", so that she had to apply firm discipline with some use of the cane before she won over their respect and support. In her view every child has an individual gift of knowledge that the teachers should identify and encourage. She recalls that the many Goodenough children were mostly good at geography, whilst the Purnells loved history: On the other hand, the Vinces liked playing ball games, whilst Nancy Hunt's daughter who had a beautiful voice used to sing all day long!

Florence soon settled down and she and Kate were to make an excellent team. Indeed, a former pupil, Richard Dunne, has said that "*they were the best teachers South Stoke has ever had*". In due course Florence was to marry Mr. Naish, who had been invalided out of the Merchant Navy. He became a craft master at the Woodcote School. They lived at Checkendon, where they brought up their three children. She is remembered by many for her motor bike on which she used to come to school. "*Yes*" says Florence, "*after I was married, I did get a motorcycle on which I would ride to school. Sometimes, when road conditions were bad, I would have to take a longer route and this could involve a round trip of some 50 miles. But I was only late twice in all of 30 years and that was due to snow. On one occasion in 1963 I tried to avoid the snow by going down Elvendon Road, (in Cleeve) but I still got stuck in a snowdrift and had to wait for someone with a tractor to come and pull me out".*

"When the roads were icy and slippery, I used to wear gloves and leggings and put socks over my shoes. They would all be frozen by the time I arrived! But the children were marvellous. They would take off my socks and leggings and, whilst I thawed out in front of the stove, would get the blackboard, desks and chairs all ready for the lessons. I often used to fill my bike with petrol at the Cross Keys garage run by Arthur Smith. He once remarked that it was not fitting for a lady to be riding a motorbike, to which I replied, "I am not a lady". Once I got to school the day would always start with Assembly, when prayers were said and a hymn was sung. Kate would then take the infants off to a separate room whilst I taught the older ones. They would each have their own desk, in which they kept their own books, pen, pencil and ruler. At the end of the day I would take their books home in a large basket, mark them and correct spelling and grammar mistakes. All the children were very good at welcoming newcomers to the school and helping them with the basics of reading and writing".

"As it was essential that these newcomers should learn to read as soon as possible, I would concentrate on this and go through the letters of the alphabet with them, giving each letter the name of a friend or relative so that they could remember easily. To start the children writing I would first have to show how to hold a pen in the right way, with the little finger remaining stationary on the paper for each word, whilst I would emphasise the necessary rhythm and flow. During the dinner break I used to write poetry on the blackboard in my best hand, for the children to copy, and would then draw a picture to illustrate it. The children would also keep special exercise books on the river, the farm, hedges, birds, flowers and the sky, in which they would record all they had seen and heard on the way to

school, and on special lessons and outings. On this they usually worked in threes, sharing the writing and drawing".

"School dinners used to be brought over from Goring by Mrs. Walters; whilst school heating was by a slow combustion stove and lighting from oil lamps. The bucket toilets were out at the back and were emptied regularly by Mr. Walters: we never had an epidemic illness during all my time! For recreation we played plenty of games, cricket and football for the boys and ball games for the girls. Then there was the swimming: it started first of all by the Four Arches bridge, but later we had a proper place below the village, with an area of water netted in.

The boom for the learner swimmers in the River Thames

I was helped by Peggy Peplar, and at first, we used to get into the river and support each child, but later we had them suspended from a long pole. We started by teaching them the dog paddle and slowly built up their confidence until they could do the breaststroke. Then Peggy would go over to the Berkshire side of the river and the children would swim right across to her. In all those years only one child never learnt to swim, and I won a cup for teaching the most children to swim".

"We did once suggest an area swimming competition, but the other local schools all declined; however, they did take part in area sports with us when we were nearly always top, though we were once beaten by Harpsden. In addition, we had a marvellous reputation for Maypole dancing. I was very fond of maths and used to love teaching that to the children, when I tried to make the times tables as exciting as possible. I also used to include geometry, something that was unheard of in those days. I loved teaching the children to sing too and we had a good reputation for that. In fact, we often did difficult pieces which other schools could not manage. Occasionally I would get a child that had a stutter, but I found that by talking very slowly to that child it would not be long before that stutter disappeared. I have mentioned Kate Costiff who helped me at school. Her mother always used to bring her round a cup of tea, until one day she didn't come, so Kate rushed home only to find she had had a stroke. I went round to see if I could help, knowing I could safely leave the children: they were very good".

"Kate finally retired at the age of 72 and I ran the school by myself for a while, until Miss Cunningham came to help me. Another thing we used to do was to put on plays in the Village Hall. Mrs. Pamela Tozer would write them and the mothers and myself made the costumes. One such play was called the Christmas Rose, in which everyone took up presents to Baby Jesus: he just cried for joy when he got the presents, and where his tears fell so the Christmas roses grew. Everybody loved it, and I remember the Police Sergeant from Goring being so touched that tears came to his eyes! Another show was Snow White and the Seven Dwarfs. Margaret Goodenough was the wicked

Queen and her husband did the special effects. The children were all word perfect. What we didn't do! After they had left some of my former pupils would come down to lean over the school railings, and only needed a nod from me to come in and join my pupils as if they had never left. I could not have asked for a better tribute", said Florence. She clearly loved her time at the school and her memories of that time are just full of love and enthusiasm.

In the Village Scrapbook (kept at Manor Farm by Mrs. Bullock) there is a rubbing of an attendance medal of 1907 and several old photos of the school and pupils. One shows a school group in the 1920s and another is of 1943; whilst there are several photos of the Swimming Club in operation in the 1940s. A Reading Mercury photo of 1966 shows the Vicar, Roy Price, presenting the Dolphin Swimming Trophy to Mrs. Naish and three pupils, Peter Lee, Richard Dixon and Pauline Kew. Another Reading Mercury photo of 1967 shows Mrs. Naish's retirement party at the Village Hall, when she was presented with a young cherry tree and £60 in recognition of her 38 years of wonderful service to the South Stoke School. Several other school group photos taken since then are in the possession of various people in the village.

Pamela (Small) Wernham 1954 to 1961:

The reminiscences of those who went to school in more recent times are very similar, though perhaps more vivid. Pamela Wernham, who is the daughter of Eric and Esther Small, was there from 1954-61. "*They were really happy times*" she says. "*Mrs. Naish always gave us so much warmth and protection, which is what one needs to provide a solid foundation for later life. I still have a great admiration for her as she, on her own, taught us all right through our school days from the infant stage up; and still had time to answer our questions. In those days she was living in Checkendon, but always managed to get to school on time, come rain, shine or snow. Sometimes, on a snowy winter's day we used to think we might be getting a day off; but no, she was always sure to turn up, though perhaps just a few minutes late!*"

Pamela goes on to say: "*I remember the day my mother gave birth to twin girls; and of my brother Robert and I, sitting on a desk with Mrs. Naish, trying to convince the whole school around us that we now had twin sisters! I was also worried over the fact that I had been making a pair of blue bootees at school for the expected new baby; and as I had so far only made one, I now found I needed another three in a hurry*". She then recalls Mrs. Naish's interest in geography, and of how the school's walls were covered with maps of England and the World. In her day, school meals were being provided, but Pamela never liked the figs and semolina that were often served up. "*To this day I cannot face figs*" she says. Like others before her, she also remembers the very cold winters and of "*frozen milk having to be thawed out by the fire in time for morning break*". Then there was "*physical education in front of the school, with only rush mats to protect our spines against the harsh tarmac*". But she has happy memories of the swimming classes, which took place 2 or 3 times a week.

"*We would walk down to the river and cross steppingstones over some streams on the way. Sometimes we tried to run across these stones but usually ended up with wet feet! At the river there was a boom in place, running some 10 yards out into the water, to provide a safe area for us to swim in. Then there was dear Mrs. Peplar holding us up until we were confident to swim on our own. But oh, the squelchy mud between our toes, when we put our feet down, was an experience of its own*". By the middle of April "*it was time to start rehearsals for the May Pole. Three children would sit on its base to stop it falling over, out would come the wind-up gramophone from the school and dancing would begin. Now, when I see my own children doing the maypole dance, I hope it is a tradition that will never be lost. There is something quite magical about it all, especially seeing the coloured ribbons being wound round the pole*". Lastly, she remembers that each day started with the children reciting their tables, before lessons began; and recalls how happy were her schooldays at South Stoke.

Miss Jane (Tidbury) Mowforth 1965 to 1976:

It is appropriate at this point to include some reminiscences from Miss Jane Tidbury (later to become Mrs. Mowforth). She came to the school in 1965 as the infant teacher, in which capacity she was to serve until 1976, with a brief spell as acting Head Mistress in 1970. For her first two years, Mrs. Naish was in charge. On her arrival Jane found that "*changes were afoot in the village; with new houses being built, and with an influx of families from a wider area*" so that the school population was quite high. But she also found that "*the old Victorian school building had few amenities. There was no modern sanitation; the coke stoves were inadequate for classroom heating; the washing up facilities were primitive, and water would only be heated on a gas ring or on the coke stoves. The school furniture moreover was mostly riddled with woodworm*". However, the managers and parents were fully aware of the situation and were actively pressing for improvements to be made. As Jane has said, "*it was thanks to their great efforts that change was to come*".

"*In 1968 modern sanitation was installed and a cloakroom was converted into a modern kitchen. Later the coke stoves were replaced with gas heating and the classroom floors were sanded and sealed. New furniture arrived and the school became a more comfortable place*". At that time, in Jane's words, "*the relationship between parents, managers and staff was most amicable. Parents often came into school with their children in the mornings for a chat, and to look at books and paintings, etc. When they came again in the afternoons, they would congregate outside the school and converse among themselves until the children came out. It became a happy meeting place in the village! As for my teaching, it was mostly done on individual lines, and I would use the radio for music and movement. Later, when we got a TV set, I was able to choose programmes of special interest. I also got together a percussion band*".

For recreation, "*sports and games were held on the Recreation Ground; for swimming instruction children were taken to local school pools; whilst walks to the river, bogey hole and along the Bridle Path were always much enjoyed. Then there were school trips to museums and other places of interest, such as Slimbridge, Windsor Castle, etc. And in some years the juniors were taken for a week to Yenworthy on Exmoor. For these trips we were able to use the minibus from Goring School*". As regards other activities, these were many and varied. "*At times the juniors gave concerts for parents and friends; whilst each year the Infant Class would join with the South Stoke Players to put on a Christmas pantomime. For instance, in December 1969 they did Mother Goose with a cast of 21; in December 1970 Red Riding Hood, with a cast of 24; and in December 1971 Babes in the Wood with a cast of 31. They were all jolly occasions, much enjoyed by players and audience alike*". In all these shows Jane played an important part on the production side.

"*On the last day of the Christmas term a party was always held for the children at the school, which was organised and catered for by the staff. By now Mr. Long was Head Teacher and was to be followed in 1970 by Mr. Romney. As the school population had increased, we were now allowed to have an additional part-time teacher. During my time Mrs. Long, Mrs. Dew, Mrs. Romney, Mrs. Miller and Mrs. Baxter all held that post: and when Mr. Romney was in charge, he used to have a Mrs. Godley come in on Friday mornings as secretarial help. The non-teaching staff in those days comprised Mrs. Walters (caretaker), Mrs. Joan Minchin (in charge of the kitchen) and Mrs. Doris Dunne (lunchtime supervisor). All these ladies were most generous with their time, both in helping out with parties and in sewing costumes for school concerts and pantomimes*".

Louisa (Small) Niland 1966 to 1977:

Next there are some detailed reminiscences from Louisa Niland (another daughter of Eric Small), who was at school from 1966-77. *"I have very detailed memories of my infant class and of our teacher Miss Tidbury. She looked so like the Queen that I often got quite confused and wondered why it was that the Queen was here in South Stoke teaching us to read and write!"*

"Every morning would start with Miss Tidbury asking us how we were, and we would always reply in the same way - 'very well thank you'. Good manners were considered most important. Then we would start work by reciting our times tables. When someone had a birthday Miss Tidbury would bring a packet of iced sweets for that child to share with the class, and everyone would sing Happy Birthday. If we were very good, Miss Tidbury would do her train impressions, by making taps and shuffles on a desk with her hands: it was always very realistic and we used to think it was wonderful. At other times she would play for us Joyce Grenfell's record of a school class, which was a great favourite and caused much merriment". Louisa also remembers that "*Miss Tidbury used to keep a supply of spare pretty flowered knickers and pants in a drawer, in case any child had a mishap. To my great embarrassment I had such a mishap one day*".

"It was a particularly bad day, because there were no spare knickers left, and I had to wear a pair of boys' Y front pants. I never wet my knickers again after that! We had a radio in our class and on Thursdays would listen to the school Church Service: we enjoyed the hymns especially and would sing them in the playground afterwards. We also enjoyed another radio programme, Singing Together, from which we learnt a new song each week. At lunchtime Mrs. Dunne and Mrs. Minchin would bring us in our meals and very good they were too; especially a chocolate pudding with chocolate sauce, which we called cluck cluck pudding and cluck cluck sauce, accompanied by many chicken impersonations and flapping of arms! Our meals were usually served by those in the Big class, and they then had priority in getting a second helping; so, when I got to the Big class, I was often a server! After lunch we had to sit for 10 minutes with "arms folded and head down - to let your meal go down", before we were allowed out to play. Of course, it seemed like an hour to us! In the playground, under the supervision of Mrs. Dunne, we would use the climbing frames or play different games".

"The school library van would call once a month, when we would change our reading books. Likewise, a coach would come to take us and the children from Ipsden school for swimming at Turner's Court. In the summer Mrs. Thynne would allow us to use her outdoor swimming pool at Lower Farm, when we would walk there, two by two, down Ferry Lane, with great excitement! When the weather was nice we might get taken for a walk down to the river, where perhaps we might get a story read to us under a tree; or we might go to the Recreation Ground for a game of football, when we would join in with the boys. We also used to enjoy country dancing at school. And once we took part in a Mediaeval Banquet with much pomp and ceremony, when we wore long dresses and cardboard hats, to which were stapled coloured scarves. I certainly look back on my schooldays with happy memories".

Head teachers, Paul Overton and Peter Smith 1979 to 1987:

Head teachers Paul Overton (1979-84) and Peter Smith (1984-87) both submitted reminiscences of their time at the school. Mr. Overton well remembers starting work in January 1979, with everything "*inches deep in snow*", so that "*my first act as head teacher was to close the school for a few days, as neither teaching staff nor school meals could reach the village*". During my tenure "*an upstairs room with external metal staircase was converted into an office for me. By now there were some 80 children on the roll and, apart from Mrs. Hopkins and Mrs. Saunders, there were two part-time staff members. These ladies were very musical and ensured that standards of singing and playing were always kept at a very high level. I also had a school secretary, Mrs. Ward, who came two days a week; whilst Doreen Druce was Caretaker and General Assistant. Mrs. Lee looked after the kitchen; and Mrs. Minchin, Hillier and Casbeard supervised the lunches*".

"*As the number of children declined, so the teaching staff was reduced until by 1981 or 1982 there was only Mrs. Saunders and myself. But we had great support and help from parents and friends in the village, especially from Mrs. Sandra Bell, Linda Gatto, Penny Luff and Glenys Wilkinson, so we were able to get by. Much of the children's work was concerned with their local environment, and we developed close links with Manor Farm. In this we had great help from Frank and Martin Bullock and their staff, and we all of us gained a greater insight into the ways of farming and country life. The children also visited places of interest further afield. I recall in particular a visit we made to a Junior School in Balham, a huge Victorian edifice in busy London. What they saw all came as a great surprise to our children. Likewise, there was a similar culture shock when the Balham children returned the visit and spent a day in South Stoke. They toured the farm and fields, had a picnic meal courtesy of Mrs. Bullock and taught our children a whole new series of playground games and rhymes*".

Otherwise Paul Overton recalls "*the inspiration the school drew from the Church*"; and of how "*Christmas carol concerts, Harvest Festivals and other special occasions were all greatly enhanced by the magic of the Church itself*". He mentions the interest in swimming and other sports and has a lot to say about local events in the school's calendar; such as "*Pancake races along the village Street, with intense competition in the Parent races!*" And of course, about the May Day activities, with the Maypole dancing, Queen of the May and the stalls and sideshows. "*Bonfire night*", he says, "*became a significant event in the PTA calendar; and I can still hear the "whoosh" which signified that David Druce and his team had persuaded the bonfire to light. During the five years that I had the pleasure of being the head teacher, all the family benefited from the way that everyone in the village made us feel welcome. The children, parents and villagers all helped to make it an experience we can never forget*".

Peter Smith remembers that he came at a time "*of great changes that were to sweep through the educational system*". On arrival he had Pam Saunders to help him as the infant teacher; but pupil numbers were now falling "*and two years later the roll was below 31 and I was the only qualified teacher in school*". However, he had as classroom assistants Doreen Druce, Hilary Barnby and Rita Mann; and with their help was able to manage and "*to provide a broad and balanced curriculum with the benefits of a rural environment*". He has described how "*the annual cycle of village events, ably run and supported by the school's PTA, ensured a regular seasonal pattern to school life which seemed to embody everything that is good in an active rural community. From Pancake Day street races through to a Christmas Nativity in the Church next door, there was always something exciting for the children and the community to look forward to. We also provided a school choir at the Church's Family Services*".

He speaks of the equipment provided for the school during his time; a TV set, video recorder, a computer, printer and disc drive; also, a lot of extra books. New bookcases and curtains were also obtained. He talks of trips to the theatre, visits to Oxford museums; "*of youth hostelling to Bath and York, and of a week spent at the Woodlands Outdoor Pursuit Centre in Wales*". However, as school numbers dropped, "*it twice came under threat of closure*", and it was only through the support of parents, governors and the whole community that this threat was averted. Pupil numbers now rose from their lowest ebb of 21, and a new infant teacher was authorised. "*By 1987 we had gone full circle, with Mrs. Hollick now in place as the new infant teacher and the school roll stable. I was able to leave South Stoke a better equipped school, ready to face the challenges of the 1990s*".

APPENDIX 3

WAR MEMORIES OF SOUTH STOKE

This appendix is part of a compilation from various sources: material in the Women's Institute Village Book; from the Happy Circle book of memories; from the Bullock family scrapbook and from personal memories of Eric Small.

In the Great War, the village lost eleven young men. These are all remembered on the village War Memorial, which was unveiled and dedicated in August 1920. After World War II two more names were added.

The Second World War broke out in September 1939; followed by the dark days of 1940, when nine of South Stoke's young men - out of the twenty seven who were to join the Forces - were to be captured during the evacuation from France, at Dunkirk and elsewhere. Several of South Stoke's young men were in agricultural employment and were not of course permitted to join up and instead had to be content with joining the Local Defence Volunteers

/Home Guard. Ivol Barn and surrounding area, being flat and open arable land, was considered a likely site for possible German parachute landings and even for planes to land on. So Eric Small was given specific responsibility for the first line defence of the area, and was issued with a Browning automatic rifle and ammunition, which he always had to keep ready at home. At nights he and other members of the local unit used to stand guard on Watch Folly, the highest hill in the parish, which lay behind Ivol Barn, and where there was a shepherd's hut with telephone; whilst by day the same post was manned by the women of the village.

Front row, fourth from left, is Eric Small

The Home Guard came into being in May of 1940. It was known initially as the Local Defence Volunteers, with members merely wearing an LDV armband over their civilian clothes, at the time that

Europe was being overrun by the German Army. After the Dunkirk evacuation of June 1940 it was known as the Home Guard. All members were volunteers, aged between 15 and 65. The aims of the Home Guard were threefold: to deal with enemy parachutists; to neutralise 5th columnists; and, in the event of enemy landings, to harass and delay their forces (especially tank columns) advancing inland from the coast. At first weapons of all sorts were in short supply, but their availability gradually improved, as did the provision of uniforms. Major Ducker of Little Stoke was the HG Area Commander.

Life was difficult in those days. Men in the village often, after a long day's work, also had to do an all-night guard; whilst routine parades and training took up many evenings and weekends. All carried out on normal civilian rations and without pay. As mentioned, a mobile telephone was connected to Watch Folly for Home Guard use; but otherwise there were in South Stoke only four telephones - at the Post Office run by Mr. Costiff, at Mr. Gibbs' house (now "Stoke Abbas"), at the Vicarage and at Colonel Thynne's house- "Panters". During that critical summer of 1940 a barrier was erected and manned at the junction of Ferry Road and the Wallingford Road, and a slit trench dug nearby for cover. As summer turned into winter and the Blitz began on London, a searchlight unit was set up at Little Stoke, and at nights the red glow of fires could clearly be seen in the direction of London.

The War Years brought many problems. In those days coal was still freely available, but petrol was becoming increasingly scarce, not that there were many cars about in South Stoke anyway (the first car only having arrived in the village in around 1912). Nonetheless Arthur Smith, who had a petrol pump at the Cross Keys Inn, never seemed to be short. However he always kept a bag of sugar handy, ready to put in his storage tank to neutralise the petrol, in the event of any German troops arriving on the scene! Soon members of the Women's Land Army began to appear in the vicinity, to help in the increasing drive for agricultural production and to replace the menfolk as they were called up.

As the war continued the big Springfield boatyard, located on the River Thames just within the South Stoke/Goring parish boundary and still serviceable, was brought into use to serve the war effort. It was utilised for the storage of foodstuffs and for their subsequent distribution to needy areas. It was ideally situated for the barge traffic to load and unload, and was used as a storage depot throughout the war years. Meanwhile, the first postcards were coming into the village, for the relatives of those concerned, with news from the German authorities of those men captured in the evacuation from France. As they were written in German no one could understand them, and they were taken up to Mr. Moore, a retired purser from the ocean liner "Aquitania" who had built himself Ashmount House just before the war, for translation. The village was now closely involved in various wartime activities. Regular National Savings drives took place: Mrs. Rouse at the Perch and Pike Inn organised the collection of aluminium utensils for aircraft manufacture. The village adopted a warship and everyone worked closely together for the common good during those years.

One of the village activities was a Blackout Competition, held during 1941/42, which led to the collection of various reminiscences of local life. The atmosphere of the village at that time was described thus: "*There is almost a dreamlike quality about the little street - so remote does it seem from the terrors of war - enclosed in its sheltered hollow, guarded on the one side by the Chilterns and on the other by the streams and marshes of the river*". In 1942/43 U.S. troops came to the area and took over the Springs Hotel (at North Stoke). They often used the old quarry above Little Stoke as a firing range, and Eric Small remembers how careless they were with ammunition, often leaving some lying behind after they had used the range. In 1942 a U.S. Army Sergeant was to get married in South Stoke; and after the war (in 1955 and 1956) two more U.S. Servicemen were to marry local girls (the Walters' daughters). As preparations for D Day began to be made in 1944 huge quantities of equipment and weapons were stockpiled in the Chiltern beech woods beyond Woodcote. Sadly, as the war drew to a close, South Stoke was to lose two of its young men, David Dill and Thomas Pither.

The former was killed behind enemy lines in Germany, whilst on a special operation in November 1944; whilst the latter was killed in an escape attempt from a German P.O.W. camp in March of 1945.

During those war years there were several particular events which occurred in the vicinity of South Stoke. In 1939 there was a tragic air accident at "Ye Leather Bottel", the inn beside the Thames, when

Pilot Officer Peter Phillips (aged 22 and son of the vicar of Moulsford) was killed. He was stationed at North Weald as part of 151 Fighter Squadron and had flown up to Benson, from where he had been visiting his parents. He then took off in his Miles Magister aircraft, together with a fellow Australian pilot, to return to North Weald in Kent. He flew low over Moulsford, to wave farewell to his parents, and in doing so circled that village and South Stoke twice. On the second occasion he appeared to get into difficulties, seemed to lose height and a wingtip then struck the roof of the riverside tavern, causing the plane to crash through the fir trees above the inn. The young pilot was to die from head injuries some 20 minutes after he was pulled from the wreckage. His Australian friend was taken to Wallingford hospital, with severe injuries, but was happily to survive.[1]

As has been mentioned before, the flat farmland around Ivol Barn was suitable for possible aircraft landings; and, apart from being a potential enemy landing zone in 1940, was later designated an emergency landing area for Allied aircraft in difficulties. Its use in this respect led to several crash landings during the war years. There was that of a Fairey Swordfish near Ivol Barn in 1940; of a Wellington bomber, which crashed on White Hill with the death of all on board in 1941; of a Halifax bomber, which came down near Ipsden Church in 1943; and of a Liberator bomber, also near Ivol Barn 1944. In the same year the area of "*the Prairies*" was also used by Allied troops to practice parachute landings. During that time Benson airfield was devoted to photographic reconnaissance, and its P.R.Spitfires and Mosquitoes were a common sight over South Stoke. The airfield at Hampstead Norreys was used by bomber aircraft (and later during D Day and thereafter for towing gliders); and during 1943/1944, as the bombing campaign against Germany intensified, bombers used to assemble in the air over South Stoke before setting off for the continent. Many villagers still remember the noise they made as the bombers would congregate overhead. On the other hand there was very little enemy activity in the area, though a lone bomber did in November 1940, drop a stick of bombs along the railway line north of the "*Temple*", on the outskirts of Goring. This did some damage and also caused the death of Mrs. Olive Fox when a bomb hit her home "*Duttons*" (or Bird Place) alongside the river. Later some bombs fell in the fields near the Four Arches railway bridge, without causing any damage. Several were unexploded and had to be blown up later. In 1941 a German plane crash landed near Cholsey, with its crew being taken prisoner.

Otherwise South Stoke suffered no enemy action. In other aspects however the effect of war was soon apparent, as identity cards, the blackout, rationing and conscription came in. Also in the early days, some 53 evacuees, together with their teachers, were to arrive in and to be distributed around the village. The only problem they caused was the overcrowding at the school! Soon of course men from the village were leaving for France to join the British Expeditionary Force. But little was happening there, and it was not until June of 1940 that the real impact of war was to hit England. South Stoke was then particularly affected since nine of its young men were to be taken prisoner during the retreat to Dunkirk and in the defence of the beach-head perimeter; and were not to come home until 5 years later. Then came the call for Local Defence Volunteers (later Home Guard); the building of blockhouses along the Thames and the other defence measures. Then followed the Battle of Britain and the Blitz, after which the country settled down to a long hard war. With the submarine blockade the need for food production was paramount, and soon everybody was "Digging for

Victory". At Manor Farm there was a change-over to the growing of sugar beet, potatoes, vegetables and wheat; with straw being used for paper production. Although the farm then used horses, the first two tractors were purchased during those years. At long last the war came to an end and the young men came home again, with a special welcome to those who had spent many years in captivity.

ENDNOTE and SOURCES:

1. *"Fatal Aeroplane Crash at South Stoke"*-Reading Mercury Saturday 5th August 1939.

For general reading regarding aircraft see:-

"British Aircraft at War 1939-1945" by Gordon Swanborough Published 1997 by HPC Publishing.

"British Aircraft of World War II" by David Mondey. Published by Chancellor Press, the re- issued edition 1994.

"The Right of the Line. The Role of the RAF in World War Two" by John Terraine. Published 2010 by Pen and Sword Military.

There are numerous websites that will lead on to further reading such as :-
http://www.historyofwar.org

A Military History Encyclopedia Website
http://www.ukairfieldguide.net/airfields/Benson

APPENDIX 4

BERKS & OXON ADVERTISER 1905

The following is a transcription of reports which appeared in the Friday 25th August 1905 edition of the newspaper reporting the fire in South Stoke which started on the 19th August:-

On Saturday afternoon the picturesque village of South Stoke was the scene of the most disastrous fire that has occurred in this neighbourhood for many years. The cause of the outbreak was no novel one: it was the old story of a boy playing with matches in a rick-yard. Mr Brock, on whose premises the fire originated, happened to be on the spot almost at the moment it commenced: but all human efforts to stay the outbreak were in vain. The farm-yard is situated at the north end of the village on the south side of Ferry Road. Half a gale was blowing from the west-south-west: had the wind been in any other quarter the whole of the village would now lie in ruins. The yard was well stacked with freshly carried corn, and in a moment was blazing with terrific intensity. The flames leapt with appalling rapidity from rick to rick: tongues of fire licked the thatched barns and farm buildings, which instantly became a mass of flames. Great flakes of burning straw and thatch were lifted by the wind, and but a few minutes after the first alarm the fire had burst out across the ferry road in the rickyard of College Farm occupied by Mr. Bullock. More valuable ricks of corn and hay and the farm buildings added fresh fuel to the devouring flames.

Within half an hour there were three farmyards ablaze, for Manor Farm, also occupied by Mr Bullock, had become alight by the shower of burning straw that was driven through the air by the fierce wind. In one barn there were 200 quarters of oats, and in all some 27 ricks were involved. In the meantime two thatched cottages close to Mr. Brock's farmyard had taken fire, and two others, standing in an isolated position and screened by a row of tall elms, were also hopelessly alight. So fierce were the flames that growing trees caught fire; a poplar burned for hours and fine elms suffered. For almost a quarter of a mile the fire continued its disastrous course. Immediately on the outbreak telegrams were despatched to neighbouring fire brigades. The Wallingford steam fire engine and brigade under Captain W Honeybone were the first to arrive on the scene some three quarters of an hour after the call. Goring and Whitchurch Brigades with a manual were in attendance about the same time and later the County Fire Office manual came over from Reading. Captain W Honeybone took command, and at once set about limiting as far as possible the spread of the conflagration. But the fire by this time had got a firm hold and covered a tremendous area. The Wallingford engine was set at work at a stream some 60 yards from the river and over 300 yards from the nearest point of the fire. Attention was first directed to the burning cottage on Mr. Brock's farm, which stood close to a thatched barn so far untouched by the flames. This they succeeded in saving, and also a tiled barn on the opposite side of the road which had already been touched by the flames. Next they deadened the ricks in Mr. Brock's farmyard, and then turned to a burning thatched outhouse only separated by three or four feet from a thatched cottage. Here again they were successful in staying the spread of the fire. In the meantime the members of the Goring Fire Brigade were working a second line of hose fed by the Wallingford engine, while some hundreds of yards away the Pangbourne and County Fire Office manuals were doing good work at the Manor Farm. Their efforts were principally devoted to saving Mr. Bullock's house and a large barn, and success attended them in each case. Naturally, the villagers were in a state of the greatest alarm. At one time the destruction of the whole village appeared imminent. In a great many cases furniture was hastily removed, and every preparation made for speedy clearance. Happily, the wind blew very much from the same point, otherwise the disaster would have been overwhelming. There is one satisfactory feature to record, and that is the saving of all livestock. The buildings and stock were fortunately covered by insurance, the policies, we understand, being effected through the Norwich Union office. It is almost impossible to speak too highly of the splendid services rendered by the Fire Brigades, or of the invaluable working of the Wallingford steam engine. Not only was it playing direct on the flames, but it kept up water in a pond to allow manuals to continue their useful work a quarter of a mile away. It is estimated, making all allowances for "stops" that the Wallingford engine poured a stream of some 600,000 gallons of water on the flames. All the brigades continued their work through the night, and kept at it for some 24 hours at a stretch. The stumps of half consumed ricks and the ruins of the farm buildings were still ablaze on Monday, and it was thought desirable to again enlist the Wallingford Brigade in the evening. The engine was again set to work, and a systematic course of action pursued. By the aid of a large chain of willing helpers the burning stacks were pulled over and exposed to the two jets from the engine. The work was continued for another 24 hours, and even some of the ruins were still smouldering in places. The scene of the fire was visited by a great number of people, and on Sunday, it is estimated that some thousands made their way to South Stoke. On that day over 1200 crossed the ferry from the *"Beetle and Wedge"*.

Another account

A writer in a contemporary says:- The most unpopular person in South Stoke, a Thames Valley village some two and a half miles from Goring, is a small boy named Strange, who on Saturday afternoon nearly succeeded in burning the place to the ground. This unhappy youth started to play with a box of matches at about four o'clock near a hayrick on Mr. Brock's farm, and when a reporter left on Monday evening the village was still burning. South Stoke's population numbers about 400 and the buildings in the village, which is chiefly owned by Christ Church College, Oxford, are for the most part thatched. The only reason why the entire village was not burnt up is that the fire started at the northern end of it, and the wind happened to be blowing west. Three farmyards were devastated - Mr. Brock's, College Farm and Manor Farm, all owned by Christ Church College. The chief damage done was the destruction of 18 cornricks, only recently got in, and valued at £6,000. Three occupied cottages, with a quantity of machinery, barns, granaries and other farm buildings and implements, bring the damage up to nearly £10,000, all of which is covered by insurance. Fortunately, the only farm dwelling house on the premises - that of Mr. Bullock, of the Manor Farm - happened to be out of the line of fire, and escaped. There was a strong wind on Saturday afternoon, so that almost before the village realised what was afoot, the fire had jumped across the road from Brock's Farm to College Farm and College Farm to Manor Farm. When the first fire brigade arrived at half past five from Wallingford, all the places, fanned by the high wind, were burning fiercely. At all three points there were exciting incidents, which will live long on the tongues of village gossips. At Brock's, where the fire started the cattle were so frightened at the haste with which they were hustled out of the cowhouse that one beast rushed at a labourer and ripped his thigh open with its horns. Doctors and nurses fortunately happened to be on the spot. Midway between Brock's and College Farm there were two tiled cottages only a yard or two out of the course of the fire, and in imminent danger therefrom. While the rest of the family were engaged in throwing the furniture out of the window the man of the house spent four distracted hours in watering a three yard space of thatch on his roof as if it were a valuable geranium that he was coaxing into bloom: and when finally forced into the open by suffocating smoke from the neighbouring granaries he rushed back again into the danger zone to rescue two tame rabbits from hutches in the back yard. Just as the fire reached the Manor Farm a waggon of corn was running down the road from the wheat field. A spark reached it and almost before the horse could be dragged out of the shafts, corn, waggon and all were blazing. A few scraps of old iron by the side of the road are all that remain of that cart and the corn that was on it. Fire brigades from Wallingford, Pangbourne, Reading and Goring were busy all Saturday night, Sunday, and Monday morning. The last left Monday afternoon, but clouds of smoke were still rising from the ruins of the ricks, and the villagers, arguing that a change in the set of the wind was the only thing needed to spread the fire over the rest of this tinder box village, had just recalled one of the brigades when our reporter left. Crowds of visitors have walked, cycled, or driven over from all parts of the compass and yesterday the Plough and Harrow was eaten out of house and home. The landlady's favourite motto now is: *"it's an ill wind that blows nobody any good"*.

LIST OF MAPS and ILLUSTRATIONS

∞---∞

END

Printed in Great Britain
by Amazon

49422630R00154